The History of Britain
AN AERIAL VIEW

The History of Britain
AN AERIAL VIEW

CHRISTOPHER STANLEY

W W Norton & Co Inc
New York · London

Cessna 150 aircraft flying over the Buckinghamshire countryside near High Wycombe
All the photographs used to illustrate this book were taken from Cessna aircraft operating from Denham airfield in Buckinghamshire. The Cessna's high wing, clear all-round visibility, and low stalling speed make it an ideal aircraft for this type of aerial photography. Several hundred flights were needed to produce the material used in this book. The aircraft was piloted on each occasion by Mr Leslie Banks.

ISBN 0-393-01944-6

Printed in Hong Kong
for the Publisher
W.W. Norton & Company Inc
500 Fifth Avenue
New York, New York 10110
First American edition 1985

CONTENTS

5

PREFACE

The only view most people have of Britain from the air is that brief glimpse from a commercial airliner taking off or landing at one of the major airports. Within minutes the view is obscured by cloud or a layer of blue haze. Taking off from London's Heathrow airport one might be rewarded with a view of Windsor Castle and the centre of London, but attempts to take a photograph are usually thwarted by a scratched or dirty window or the shimmer of heat from the jet engine's exhaust. The resulting photograph is usually only of personal interest.

The photographs used to illustrate this book are the result of several hundred hours' flying using high-wing Cessna aircraft based at Denham Aerodrome in Buckinghamshire. The pilot on each occasion was Mr Leslie Banks to whom I owe a deep debt of gratitude. His skilled airmanship and his navigational ability in pinpointing a small field in what seems like the middle of nowhere are quite outstanding.

Flying was carried out at all times of the year, because the number of days when conditions are ideal for aerial photography is very limited. To produce really clear photographs free from any trace of haze, a horizontal visibility in excess of 50 kilometres is required. This usually occurs behind a showery airstream. On many occasions we made flights to sites several hundred kilometres distant, only to find them obscured by a dark cloud which obstinately refused to move. But if there were the occasional frustrating moments, these were more than matched by superb conditions which exceeded even our wildest expectations. Here mention must be made of some of the photographs of the Roman town of Silchester, which it has only been possible to take so effectively on one half-day during the last 25 years, and which may never be repeated. In these pictures, not only the Roman street system, but also the outline plans of the Roman buildings are clearly visible as a height differential in a crop of ripening barley. During the previous week when the crop was developing the weather was cloudy. On the next clear day the photographs were taken, but during the operation a violent thunderstorm approached from the west. The aircraft was flown to the south to avoid it and on our return half-an-hour later the crop had been completely flattened by the heavy rain. Since then a change in the agricultural use of the land has made it extremely unlikely that any similar photographs could be taken in the foreseeable future.

Searching for lost archaeological sites is one of the most rewarding aspects of aerial photography. Time and again one can fly over an area but only if conditions are exactly right will anything be revealed in the fields below. Then it may be possible to detect anything from a prehistoric burial site to a twentieth-century gas main, and deciding what a particular photograph represents may call for skilled interpretation. It was whilst searching for archaeological sites that I first realized the potential of studying other periods of history from the air. Accordingly I began to build up a broader collection of photographs that I felt were of historical interest. Some of these are brought together for the first time in this book.

Most of the photographs were taken using a 35mm reflex camera with a through-the-lens metering facility. Initially a series of interchangeable lenses were used but recently these have been changed in favour of a 70–150mm zoom lens. A fine-grain colour transparency film has been used wherever possible. This type of film has the disadvantage of a slow speed which limits its use to days when there is bright sunlight. Some compromise has to be accepted during the winter months. The speed of the aircraft is about 120km/hour. This means that the camera has to be set with a fast shutter speed in order to prevent a blurred picture. An exposure of 1/500 second is usually required although in stable air with very little turbulence, it is sometimes possible to use 1/250 second. Picture composition is a skilled business as a decision has to be taken in a fraction of a second.

Although some flying is done on a speculative basis, in most cases the aircraft is flown to pre-determined points on a plan using a course plotted over the shortest feasible distance. Most of the target areas are visited on the ground beforehand. A note is made of their position, the time of day when the light will provide the best contrast, and the angle of approach of the aircraft in order to obtain the best view. It saves a considerable amount of time and money if it is possible to take the photograph on one fly-past. This is an ideal situation however, and works well when the subject to be photographed is large enough to be easily identifiable from a distance, such as a castle or a country house. If it is necessary to do a circuit at, say, a greater height in order to show a larger area, this will take up about three minutes' flying time. Although three minutes might not seem very long, a few such circuits in an hour use up valuable time that could usefully be deployed elsewhere. For smaller targets like an open field or a small building, finding the actual location can prove more difficult. From above things look very different; in addition the flying is sometimes so precise, that what we are looking for is found to be immediately underneath the aircraft and hidden from view!

In the search for archaeological sites, there is often no chance of a repeat flight and the hardest discipline is to know exactly where you are at any instant of time. Knowing your location to a few fields' distance is absolutely no use at all. One often starts with the best intentions, but it is quite easy to be side-tracked by another site nearby, change course and photograph it. However there is no point in having a collection of photographs, no matter how good, if their precise subject or location is unknown.

The photographs used to illustrate this book represent only a small fraction of those in my collection. It is hoped that you will have as much pleasure looking at the pictures as I had in taking them.

C. C. Stanley
1984

INTRODUCTION

Looking down on the British landscape from a height of around 1500 feet, it is possible to obtain a unique insight into its history and development over the last 5000 years. The position of the towns and villages, the pattern of the road system, and the shape of the fields, all reveal a story that began when ancient man first ceased his nomadic existence, and began to form settled communities and systematically clear and cultivate the countryside around him. It is a story interspersed with tribal rivalries, skirmishes and even wars which resulted in the construction of forts, castles and defended manor houses designed to protect their occupants in times of strife.

Many towns and cities have their origins in the Roman period and in some cases even earlier than that, whilst the layout of some medieval towns reflects earlier patterns of agriculture. The owners of the great stately homes often commissioned landscape gardening on the grand scale with ornamental parks, sometimes covering several hundred acres. Some of the greatest changes were brought about by the Industrial Revolution in the early nineteenth century whilst today the pace of change is accelerating – the result of the introduction of heavy earthmoving equipment and the use of cement and concrete as building materials.

Most of the earliest remains visible from ground level are of a religious nature – stone circles and burial mounds, all trace of the houses in which people lived having vanished thousands of years ago, covered now with a considerable depth of soil. However, their outline plans can still be detected in fields when the crops are beginning to ripen, given the right conditions: though these are almost invisible at ground level the patterns can be detected from an aircraft flying above. By using aerial techniques first pioneered in the early 1920s much can thus be learnt about Britain's hidden history. This approach is particularly rewarding in the study of Roman Britain where in some instances the outline of an entire town plan including the streets and buildings becomes visible.

Aerial photography is also useful in the study of standing monuments. It enables a site to be seen in its context. The military significance of castles can be more clearly understood. The landscape gardens of country houses can be seen as they must once have appeared in the minds of their designers, who were never fortunate enough to have such a view. One aerial photograph can often convey as much information as a hundred taken at ground level.

Sometimes, viewing sites from the air, it is difficult to obtain an idea of scale; difficult to imagine, with a prehistoric stone circle like Avebury, how thousands of cubic metres of earth and rock were dug by ancient man using a pick made from an antler and a shovel from the shoulder blade of an ox.

The changes that started with the first Stone Age farmers were continued during the Bronze Age when metal was taking the place of flint for implements and weapons. The most noticeable evidence of this period is the many circular burial mounds or round barrows often marked on Ordnance Survey maps as tumuli. Only a small fraction of those once constructed still survive today. Many others on good arable land were ploughed flat several centuries ago, but their presence can often still be detected from the air.

During the Iron Age which began about 500 BC on the introduction of that metal from the continent of Europe, a series of hillforts was constructed on prominent hills in Britain. They consisted of one or a number of banks and ditches that followed the contours around a hilltop. Very few were permanently inhabited. People tended to move into them in times of strife and at other times farmed the surrounding countryside. Aerial photography has transformed our knowledge of the Iron Age. Settlements and farmsteads have been discovered in the valleys and alongside the rivers which were totally unknown before the advent of the technique, and more are being found whenever climatic conditions are suitable.

The remains of four centuries of Roman life are also numerous. Apart from the towns, road systems and certain standing monuments such as Hadrian's Wall, forts and amphitheatres, and many hitherto unknown villas or farmsteads have been located from the air, greatly adding to our knowledge of the Roman way of life. The period after the decline of Roman Britain, known popularly as the Dark Ages, because of a general lack of evidence in records or

archaeological excavation, is less well reflected in aerial photography. Few sites of this period have been located from the air, or if they have, they have not been identified as such.

Undoubtedly some villages have a Saxon origin but it is for the period after the Norman invasion of William the Conqueror in 1066 and the Battle of Hastings that there is a wealth of subjects to photograph from the air. In order to maintain a hold on his newly won kingdom, William built several hundred castles around the countryside at strategic points. The first castles were simple earthwork structures, often surrounded by timber palisades with circular or square wooden keeps built on a natural, or more often artificial, mound known as the 'motte'. In the twelfth and thirteenth centuries the timber walls were replaced by stone and the castle developed into the type of structure we usually associate with the word.

By the mid-fourteenth century the castle was being replaced by the manor house as a more comfortable place in which to live. Because of the occasional threats of invasion from France and Spain, the owners of some manor houses were given by the King a licence to 'crenellate', or fortify, their houses. Some owners inter-

The changing English landscape

An aerial view of the Yorkshire countryside looking west from a point close to Sutton Bank provides an interesting insight into the English landscape. The position of the villages, the pattern of the road system and the layout and shape of the fields reflect a changing pattern which has slowly evolved to its present form over a period of several thousand years. The process began when ancient man first ceased his nomadic existence, began to form settled communities and systematically farmed the countryside around him.

preted this very liberally; a number of manor houses were made to look like castles, and are often known as such.

For the first half of the present millennium, religion played a part in the spiritual, economic and social life of the community in a way many find difficult to imagine today. The fact is reflected in the other great architectural tradition of the medieval period – the building of churches and cathedrals. Britain's parish churches are among its inherited glories, but perhaps more spectacular from above are the great cathedrals, sometimes, like York Minster, surrounded by a maze of streets still recognizably medieval in feeling, sometimes, like St Paul's, standing in splendid isolation amid the undistinguished products of the modern age of building. From the air the cathedral's setting can be readily appreciated, and many people are surprised to see that the flying buttresses of St Paul's are cleverly concealed from the observer at ground level.

Medieval village life was subject to radical changes. Village populations, already reduced by the effects of the Black Death, were affected by alterations in the climate. During the fourteenth century the weather became wetter, crops failed and much land under cultivation was abandoned as unworkable. Increases in sheep farming as landowners were tempted by the high price of wool also resulted in much arable land being turned into pasture. As fewer people were required to tend the sheep the villages were gradually deserted. It has been estimated that over 2000 villages in England were abandoned for this and other reasons during the Middle Ages. Many of these deserted-village sites have been located through aerial photography.

From the time of King Henry VIII a number of large and beautiful manor houses were constructed. Tudor architecture still retained a

semblance of the Gothic style carried over from the previous century, indeed some Gothic characteristics persisted into the seventeenth century. Large Tudor houses were built round a quadrangular courtyard entered through a gatehouse. The gatehouse often had a fortified appearance and battlemented parapets. Towers and turrets lingered on for ornament rather than defence. The presence of ornamental chimneys signified comfort within. Attention was also beginning to focus on gardens which were now tending to be simply landscaped. Henry VIII indulged in a small flurry of castle building in order to protect the south-coast ports from attack from France and Spain, particularly after his disagreements with the Pope led him into the dissolution of the monasteries. The crumbling remains of some of the abbeys make interesting subjects for aerial photography.

From the Elizabethan period country houses continued to increase in stature and landscape gardening in its degree of sophistication. Elizabethan and Jacobean houses were notable for their height, huge windows and distinctive skylines, with carved brick and stone, crenellation and balustrading.

Britain's architectural heritage owes much to Inigo Jones, who had previously worked in Italy and was deeply influenced by the classical tradition, and Christopher Wren, best known for works including St Paul's Cathedral and his City of London churches, in which he adapted the baroque idiom to the English taste. Amongst his other works, the additions to Hampton Court Palace and Greenwich are particularly noteworthy. Followers of Wren included Nicholas Hawksmoor and Sir John Vanbrugh who developed an interest in the great country houses and developed a more openly baroque style.

The Georgian age was the high point of

'natural' garden construction. It was the age of Lancelot ('Capability') Brown and Humphry Repton. The symbol of Georgian wealth and power was the elegant country mansion set in acres of carefully landscaped parkland. Classical antiquity crept into architecture as it was the custom for the nobility to complete their education with a few years travel to the Continent where they visited archaeological sites. The immortal Robert Adam worked on houses such as Syon House, completely transforming the interior in a luxurious classical style. It was also a great era of town planning, as exemplified in Regency Bath, where people flocked to take the mineral waters first exploited many years earlier by the Romans.

Then came the Victorian era and with it a strange diversity of architectural styles: one foot in the future, the other in fairyland. British architecture underwent an upheaval from which some critics say it has never recovered. The enormous material expansion and the far-reaching effects of the Industrial Revolution resulting from new energy sources such as steam, gas and electricity, completely changed traditional patterns of life.

With the twentieth century came more severely functional architecture. As costs of labour began to rise the embellishments which had adorned buildings over the centuries were gradually omitted from designs. There was widespread use of concrete which enabled any form to be readily created in a type of artificial stone. American architectural styles spread across the Atlantic and there was prefabrication in building. The twentieth century saw the development of new towns. The latest of these, Milton Keynes in North Buckinghamshire, is still being developed.

The changing pattern of Britain's history can readily be appreciated from the air, and I hope that the reader will derive interest and pleasure from the sequence of pictures that follows and be encouraged to visit many of these places, photographed here from an unfamiliar and revealing angle.

1 Windmill Hill Causewayed Camp, Wiltshire

In about 3000 BC southern England was colonized by the first farming communities, who came from the continent of Europe. They brought with them the art of growing grain and breeding cattle. This marked the end of the nomadic lifestyle that had been followed hitherto in England. They settled on Windmill Hill, as it is now known, and some five centuries later the hilltop was surrounded by three roughly concentric ditches. This is one of the earliest permanent sites established in Britain. It is known as a 'causewayed camp' since the ditches are not continuous but interrupted by numerous gaps, or causeways. The exact purpose of the site is unknown, but from traces of camp fires, pottery and animal bones found in the ditches, it has been deduced that parties of herdsmen probably sheltered in them for a short period each year, whilst cattle were being rounded up from the surrounding countryside. The centre circle can clearly be seen in the photograph together with parts of the two outer circles. The small circles within the earthworks are the remains of Bronze Age round barrows or burial mounds, built many years after the site was abandoned. They date from 1600–1200 BC.

2 Belas Knap Chambered Long Barrow, Gloucestershire

Communal burial was the common practice during the Late Stone Age. Over their dead the people raised large mounds of earth which are known as 'long barrows'. Belas Knap is a particularly interesting example because it has a false entrance presumably designed to deter tomb robbers. This can be seen in the foreground. The actual entrances can be seen about half-way along the side of the mound. Inside the barrow are stone-lined chambers in which at least 38 skeletons have been found. Several skulls appear to have been dealt a heavy blow just before, or soon after death. The barrow is 53m (174ft) long and 18.3m (60ft) wide at its broader end. The burial mound is thought to date from around 2000 BC.

3 Prehistoric Cemetery, Winterbourne Stoke, Wiltshire

This is an excellent example of a prehistoric cemetery: it includes every type of burial mound. In the foreground is a Late Stone Age long barrow which seems to have influenced the siting of the circular burial mounds or round barrows at a later period, during the Bronze Age. The round barrows were made by marking out a circle. A body, or cremated remains, was then placed at its centre. Material from the edge of the circle was dug out and piled up in the centre in much the same way as children make a sandcastle on a beach. The most common form of round barrow is the 'bowl barrow', a simple circular mound with a ditch immediately outside its edge. The same type of burial custom continued throughout the Bronze Age. This

cemetery also includes 'bell barrows', large mounds separated from the surrounding ditch by a flat platform. They usually contain the burials of men sometimes accompanied by weapons and ornaments which suggest that they were warrior-chieftains. 'Disc barrows' usually contain female burials. They consist of a flat circular area surrounded by a ditch with a bank outside it, only a small mound at the centre marking the actual burial.

4 Lambourn 'Seven Barrows', Berkshire

This is one of the finest Bronze Age barrow cemeteries in England. 'Seven' is a misnomer, for there are actually at least 26 burial mounds in the group. The aerial photograph shows the central part of the group and includes a rather unusual double barrow surrounded by an oval ditch. The bones of an ox and a dog were found in one of the two mounds. The cemetery was in use between about 1750 and 800 BC.

LEFT

5 Cropmarks of Bronze Age Barrows, Crowmarsh, North Stoke, Oxfordshire

Many Bronze Age burial mounds situated on good farming land have been continually ploughed for centuries, and today all trace of them has completely disappeared – or so it seems at ground level. Photographed in midsummer when the wheat crop is in the process of ripening, the outline of the ditches which once surrounded the barrows are clearly visible as areas where the crop is still green. This is partly due to the ditches' greater soil and moisture content than the adjacent ground; this tends to retard the ripening process for a few days. The area also contains a number of multiple circles and a pair of parallel lines, the exact purpose of which is uncertain.

ABOVE

6 Foxley Farm, Eynsham, Oxfordshire

The fields surrounding Foxley Farm contain one of the most complex group of cropmarks known in Britain. This photograph shows a small section of a prehistoric cemetery, no trace of which can be seen at ground level. In addition to colour differences the crop is growing taller over the buried features. Photographed with the sun low on the horizon these marks stand out, much as the undulations of a road surface are thrown into relief by a car's headlights at night. The most prominent feature is thought to be a Late Stone Age long barrow with a round barrow at each end. There are also trackways, and the outline of what are probably huts and other traces of occupation which may be as late as Roman in origin.

7 Silbury Hill, Wiltshire

This is the largest ancient man-made mound in Europe. Despite several excavations its exact purpose remains a mystery. It was once thought to be a giant burial mound but no trace of a burial has ever been found within it. The volume of earth in the mound is about 354,000 cubic metres (12½ million cubic feet). This represents the equivalent of one bucket of soil for every man, woman and child in the present-day population of Britain. Material excavated from the mound has been found to date from about 2000 BC.

It is thought to have been a prehistoric temple and, like that of some cathedrals of more recent date, its construction seems to have spanned several centuries. The earliest phase, in about 2200 BC, consisted of digging the large circular ditch with an entrance on the north-east side. There was a bank on the inside of the ditch, of which only a slight trace now remains; and inside this, a ring of 56 pits, which are just visible here as white spots. The purpose of these pits is not known, though it is clear that they never had posts or stones standing in them. They must have had a special significance since many of them were later filled with cremated human bones. In the second phase the entrance was widened and an avenue was constructed to link Stonehenge with the nearby River Avon. The avenue is hardly visible at ground level but from the air is highlighted by shadows cast by the rising sun, and can be seen leading into the distance at the top of the picture.

It was also during this phase that the 'bluestones' were brought to the site from Dyfed in south-west Wales. After more than half of them had been erected in a double circle the builders changed their minds and dismantled them.

The third phase of construction dates from about 1600–1300 BC when local sarsen stones were brought from the nearby Marlborough downs. They were dressed into shape on site and when the upright stones had been positioned the lintels were lifted into place. They represent the finest phase of Stonehenge's construction. Subsequently a number of the larger bluestones were selected from those already used in the second phase of construction. These were carefully shaped and set up, after some rearrangement, in the plan of a horseshoe.

Although Stonehenge was undoubtedly an important religious site, its exact use will probably never be known.

8 Grimspound, Dartmoor, Devon

The remains of a Bronze Age village settlement are surrounded by a stone boundary wall enclosing an area of about 1.6 hectares (4 acres). The wall was constructed from locally occurring granite rock with large facing stones and a rubble core. The entrance to the settlement can be seen in the foreground. There were 24 circular beehive-shaped dwellings within the enclosure. The huts have a diameter of 4.5m (15ft). The walls are made of stone and the roofs, of which no trace remains, would probably have been of timber, thatch and turf. Many of the huts are overgrown with heather but traces of some of them can still be seen from the air. The settlement was built near a stream, part of which flowed through the compound. The enclosure probably provided the flocks and herds with protection at night from marauding wild animals.

RIGHT
9 Stonehenge, Wiltshire

Stonehenge is perhaps the most famous prehistoric site in Europe. It was the first archaeological site in Britain to be photographed from the air – from a balloon in 1906. Between the two World Wars many photographs were taken of the site by the RAF as practice for aerial reconnaissance. As a result Stonehenge has probably been photographed from the air more than any other ancient site.

10 Avebury, Wiltshire

Though not as well known as Stonehenge, Avebury is one of the largest prehistoric ceremonial monuments in Europe. It was built towards the end of the Stone Age when bronze implements were coming into use. Avebury is so large that although the scale is difficult to appreciate from ground level, it shows up well from the air. The vast ditch and rampart that surround the stone circle, with the village of Avebury at its centre, are over 420m (1400ft) in diameter. There were once a hundred massive unhewn stones in this circle but over the centuries many have been broken up and removed for use in local walls and farm buildings. Inside the circle were several smaller rings of upright stones. Avebury was a major engineering achievement of its period.

11 Rollright Stones, Oxfordshire

This prehistoric stone circle is thought to date from around 2000–1800 BC. Local tradition insists that the number of stones cannot be counted. This would appear to be borne out by several publications which give the number as 11! With the advantage of an aerial photograph the reader will be able to reach his own conclusion. The circle has a diameter of 30m (100ft).

12 Arbor Low, Derbyshire

Sometimes described as the 'Stonehenge of the North', Arbor Low consists of a circular bank of limestone rubble 2.2m (7ft) high and 76m (250ft) in diameter which encloses a ditch 9m (30ft) wide and 2m (6ft) deep. There are two entrances through the bank. These lead to a central plateau on which there lie 46 large limestone slabs and 13 smaller stones forming a circle. There is also a group of four stones in the middle of the monument. Unlike Stonehenge, it is probable that most of these stones were never in the upright position as excavations have not revealed any socket holes in the bedrock in which the stones would have been fixed. Arbor Low was probably constructed around 2000–1600 BC. Impingeing on the bank (foreground) is a round barrow dating from 1600–1400 BC. The purpose for which Arbor Low and other henge monuments were built is unknown. Whilst archaeologists agree that henges formed important gathering places for the people living around them, opinions differ about the activities that took place there. They may have had a religious or tribal significance.

24

LEFT

13 Cissbury Ring, Sussex

Cissbury Ring is an Iron Age hillfort on the Sussex downs. The bank and ditch enclose an area of 24.2 hectares (60 acres) and were constructed around 250 BC. The ground-surface undulations within the ramparts in the foreground are the remains of some of man's first mining activities which took place here earlier in the Stone Age, around 2500–2000 BC. Over 200 mine shafts go down, in places more than 12.2m (40ft). They were dug to extract the flints necessary for making both tools and weapons. The shafts cut through six or seven seams of flint and a series of galleries radiates horizontally from the shafts to exploit these seams.

14 Trundle Hill, Sussex

This is an octagonal Iron Age hillfort built in a commanding position and consisting of a stout bank with an outer ditch and a smaller counter-scarp bank. Just visible in the centre of this hillfort is the faint outline of an inner ditch, the remains of a Late Stone Age causewayed camp. The ditch is enhanced by the shadow produced by the setting sun and is almost invisible at ground level. The photograph was taken during a very dry summer and the grass has been parched brown. The causewayed camp dates from about 2500 BC. The hillfort was constructed during the period 250–50 BC.

15 Badbury Rings, Dorset

A steep hilltop was strengthened here with three tiers of banks and ditches during the Iron Age, in about the second century BC. Later, during the Roman period, there was probably a settlement either within the Iron Age fort or close by, as this is the meeting point of two important Roman roads. The line running almost vertically up the right-hand side of the photograph and just touching the outer bank of the fort, is Ackling Dyke, the Roman road from Old Sarum to Dorchester; whilst the diagonal field boundary in the bottom left of the picture is the Roman road from Bath to Poole Harbour. Today Badbury Rings is a popular beauty spot and the banks of the hillfort are rapidly being worn away by the patter of innumerable feet.

16 Ladle Hill, Hampshire

This is an unusual example of an Iron Age hillfort in which the early stages of construction can be studied. The fort was begun by utilizing a late Bronze Age boundary ditch which can be seen continuing from the field towards the fort, where it was enlarged and incorporated into the main ditch. The rest of the fort was then marked out and the digging carried out by gangs of men working in sections. The sections of ditch can clearly be distinguished here. The earthen rampart was to have been piled up behind the ditch. In this photograph, taken with the sun low in the sky, the heaps of earth dug out of the ditch can be seen scattered inside the fort. The sudden scare in response to which this fort was constructed must have passed quickly, for the fort was never completed.

17 Beacon Hill, Hampshire

An Iron Age hillfort, hourglass in shape, Beacon Hill has defences that consist of a bank, ditch and counterscarp bank enclosing an area of 4.9 hectares (12 acres). A number of hut circles have been discovered inside this fort indicating that it may have been permanently occupied, unlike many others which are thought to have to have been inhabited chiefly during times of strife. The small rectangle in the corner marks the grave of Lord Caernarvon who with Howard Carter discovered the tomb of Tutankhamun in Egypt in 1922.

18 Figsbury Ring, Wiltshire

An unusual feature of this large Iron Age hillfort is the inner ditch some distance inside the outer bank and ditch. The exact purpose is uncertain but it is known that the material excavated from it provided more chalk for the main bank. Excavations carried out on the site have shown that the outer bank was twice increased in height. No traces of permanent occupation have been found within the fort which is thought to have been constructed in the third century BC. Some idea of scale can be gained from the cattle seen in this photograph grazing in the centre of the earthwork in front of the two trees.

RIGHT
19 Maiden Castle, Dorset

Here one can see the vastness of the earthen ramparts of Maiden Castle; this Iron Age hillfort is the largest in Britain. In the late Stone Age there was a settlement here. For 1500 years it appears to have been deserted and then in the fifth century BC it was again occupied. The defences were strengthened on several occasions but to no avail. Shortly after the Roman invasion of Britain the fort was captured by Vespasian's Second Legion. Evidence of the battle which took place was brought to light by excavations carried out on the site by Sir Mortimer Wheeler in 1934. The complex entrances to the fort are particularly noteworthy.

20 Iron Age Farm Reconstruction, Butser Hill, Hampshire

For many years it was assumed that people in the Iron Age lived all their lives in hillforts, but largely as a result of archaeological aerial photography, many settlements have since been discovered. It is now known that people spent much of their time farming the countryside of Britain and resorted to living in hillforts only during brief troubled periods. In the Queen Elizabeth Country Park to the south of Butser Hill a scientific research project is being carried out to give archaeologists a clearer picture of life during the Iron Age. A farm has been constructed: cereals are grown and harvested and some of the nearest living relatives of the prehistoric sheep and cattle are kept. The farm is not unlike small native settlements to be found in parts of Africa at the present time. Notice the hut, the fence and surrounding ditch and the food-storage pits in which the grain was kept through the winter months. Compare this with Plate 21, which shows a cropmark of an original Iron Age farm.

21 Cropmark of an Iron Age Farmstead, Dorney, Buckinghamshire

Situated close to the River Thames, the remains of an Iron Age farmstead are almost 2m (6ft) below the ground surface at this point and yet can be detected by changes in the height and colour of the ripening crop of barley growing above. The farmstead would have looked very similar to that in the previous picture. Being close to the river, at certain times of the year it would have become very muddy underfoot. A layer of flints was therefore laid and compacted over the ground surface, and this has produced the light colour in the crop.

22 Carn Euny, Cornwall

An example of an Iron Age village, Carn Euny was in use from the first century BC until the first century AD. An interesting feature is the 'fogou' or underground dwelling consisting of a stone-lined tunnel 20m (66ft) long and 2m (6ft) high leading to a circular chamber via a side passage, whilst the main entrance leads out of one of the huts and can clearly be seen in the foreground. When this fogou was excavated it was found to be paved and fitted with drains, and represents an advanced design in terms of Iron Age house construction.

23 Iron Age Settlement, Long Wittenham, Oxfordshire

This is a crop mark of a settlement thought to date from the Iron Age; it was established on an 'island' in the middle of the River Thames. The river has since altered its course and the traces of the earlier channel can be seen as a dark green strip on the right of the picture. The settlement comprises hut circles, storage pits and enclosures. A particularly interesting feature is the row of dots running across the lower part of the picture. This is known as a 'pit-alignment'. Its exact purpose is uncertain but it is likely that the dots may represent the post holes of vertical supports for a palisade.

RIGHT
24 Silchester, Hampshire

After the decline of the Roman Empire some towns fell into a state of decay and were demolished or robbed for building stone, the land eventually being returned to agriculture. Silchester, the Roman town of Calleva Atrebatum, is one such example. All that can be seen at ground level is the stone-and-concrete wall still standing in places to a height of over 5m (16ft) and enclosing an area of 43 hectares (106 acres). A considerable amount is known about the town as a result of excavations carried out for nearly 20 years beginning in 1890, but aerial photography has considerably added to this information. In this illustration the rectangular grid pattern of the Roman street system can be seen showing up as a light colour in the ripening crop within the polygonal outline of the town wall.

25 Silchester, Hampshire: the Forum and Basilica

This photograph clearly emphasizes the importance of aerial photography as an aid to archaeology. The growth of the crop of barley has been stunted over the top of the Roman walls and their presence is revealed as a shadow. The Forum was built around a piazza 43m (142ft) x 40m (130ft). On three sides porticoes gave access to a range of rooms behind them, the square shape of which can easily be seen. The fourth side was enclosed by the Basilica, a large hall 71m (233ft) long and 18m (58ft) wide. At the right-hand end of the hall is a semi-circular wall. The Forum Basilica was the chief public building in a Roman town. The Forum served as the market place whilst the Basilica is assumed to have been the town hall.

BELOW LEFT

26 Silchester, Hampshire: Forum and Basilica Excavations, 1982

Excavations carried out on the Basilica by Reading University have shed new light on its function. It is generally thought that the Basilica was the seat of administration in a Roman town. Whatever its purpose might have been in the second century AD, it is now clear that this Basilica was used as an industrial iron-working site from the mid-third century AD.

RIGHT

27 Silchester, Hampshire: the Circular Temple

This view of the town shows a number of buildings and part of the road system. The most prominent feature is the double circle, actually a 16-sided temple. The faint diagonal lines which can be seen on parts of the photograph are thought to be the outlines of the excavation trenches dug by Victorian antiquaries.

28 Silchester, Hampshire: the Inn

The second largest building known to have existed in this Roman town covers an area almost as large as the Forum and must have been a building of considerable importance. It consists of a number of rooms arranged in three wings around a colonnaded courtyard measuring 45m (148ft) x 35m (115ft), with what seems to be a corridor running along the outside of the rooms. Although the building might have been the residence of some notable citizen, it is considered more likely to have been a *mansio* or inn.

RIGHT
29 Caerwent, Gwent, South Wales

Caerwent is one of the finest Roman monuments in Wales. It was once the Roman town of Venta Silurum. The town wall is rectangular in plan and still stands to a height of almost three metres, enclosing an area of 16.2 hectares (44 acres). The town is thought to have been founded in about 75 AD, although the wall was probably constructed more than a century and a half later. When the wall was built the citizens would have felt well protected, but a hundred years later the influence of Rome was becoming weaker and Irish raiders began to ravage towns near the coast. To counter this new threat, the defences were strengthened and a series of polygonal bastions was added along the north and south walls. These provided flanking fire against an enemy approaching the wall. The town was divided in half by a main street running west to east on the line of the present road. There were two other roads running west to east and four running north and south. In this way the town was divided up into 20 blocks or 'insulae', and the main civic buildings, the Forum and Basilica, were situated in the centre of the town, to the right of the 'Y' shaped road junction.

30 Alchester Roman Town, Oxfordshire

Although this town has not yet been excavated a considerable amount can be learnt from aerial photography. It was a rectangular walled town with four major streets meeting at the centre. The Roman Forum can be seen in the top left-hand section near the crossroads. On the opposite side of the street is a row of dots which was probably a colonnade. In the top right-hand section are some square buildings which might be temples. The outlines of some buildings are revealed by increases in the growth of the crop whilst others show up where the growth has been stunted. It is possible therefore to gain some idea of the construction. Where the crop is growing taller the buildings would have been constructed on the sleeper beam system, where a trench was dug and a large piece of timber placed in it to act as a foundation on which the wall was built. The trench has retained more soil and moisture causing a lush growth of crop. Where stone foundations were used the crop growth is retarded.

RIGHT
31 Littlecote Roman Villa, Wiltshire

This villa was first discovered in 1727–28 but its exact location was not recorded when the excavation was back-filled. It was rediscovered and excavated in 1977. When this photograph was taken the most important part of the villa was unfortunately hidden from view underneath the tented structure. The excavation revealed, in what is thought to be an early example of an 'Orphic' church, a magnificent mosaic of Orpheus surrounded by female figures accompanied by wild beasts which represent the cycle from birth to death. The site is thought to date from 180–390 AD. The villa has now been restored and is open to the public.

32 Roman Villa, Hambleden, Buckinghamshire

In a field close to the River Thames is the Hambleden Roman Villa. The term 'villa' is used loosely to describe most Roman houses and this was in fact a farm. It was excavated in 1912 and has since been reburied. Today it is only occasionally visible, as an outline in the crop of ripening corn. The rectangle in the foreground is the outline of a building associated with the farm. The dark green patches in the crop indicate former river channels. A mystery surrounds the site, for the excavation revealed a total of 97 infant burials adjacent to the villa. Their existence has never been satisfactorily explained.

33 Fishbourne Roman Palace, West Sussex

The Fishbourne Roman Palace is one of the most important Roman buildings ever to have been found in Britain. It came to light in 1960 when workmen were excavating a trench for a water main. After a decade of excavation a building was erected over part of the northern wing in order to display some of the beautiful mosaic floors. The outline of part of the eastern wing has been marked out on the ground surface. During the excavation, foundations of the Roman flower beds were discovered and today the gardens have been laid out as they were during the Roman period. The palace was roughly square in shape and constructed around the four sides of the formal garden. Only a small part has been excavated for much of it still lies buried beneath the road and the buildings in the foreground.

34 Roman Amphitheatre, Caerleon, Gwent, South Wales

Caerleon was a Roman military fortress, garrisoned by the Second Augustan Legion. Outside the south-west corner of the fort is the amphitheatre, the finest and best-preserved in Britain. It is a stone-built oval structure surrounded by a seating bank and eight vaulted entrances. At two of the entrances there are the remains of boxes for important spectators (of whom the camp commandant was probably one), and there was accommodation for between 5200 and 6000 spectators. Because a Legion normally consisted of 6000 men it has been suggested that the main purpose of this amphitheatre was to serve as a training ground for regimental drill and sword exercises. A close inspection however revealed that beast-dens etc. were provided from the outset. We may be sure that the bloody and degrading spectacles for which the Romans were famous were carried out here in addition to any other functions that may have taken place. The amphitheatre was constructed in the first century AD and continued in use with minor alterations until the end of the third century AD. It was excavated in 1926 by Sir Mortimer Wheeler.

35 Roman Amphitheatre, Dorchester, Dorset

Most civilian towns also had amphitheatres. Dorchester was the Roman town of Durnovaria. This amphitheatre was adapted by the Romans from Maumbury Rings, a Stone Age stone circle. Unlike Caerleon, it was just a simple earth construction; banks and entrances were revetted with timber walls. Long after the Roman period, it was still being used in the Middle Ages for bull, bear and badger baiting. Still later, during the Civil War in the seventeenth century, it was fortified with gun emplacements.

36 Roman Theatre, St Albans, Hertfordshire

On the edge of St Albans is much evidence of the Roman town of Verulamium. One of the most interesting sites is the second-century theatre which stood alongside Watling Street. The theatre, where plays were performed, was much rarer than the amphitheatre. Only three examples are known in Roman Britain, and only that at St Albans is anything like complete. Seating for about 1600 people was arranged around the curved bank of the auditorium. The central area might have been used for gladiatorial sports and behind this is the stage with a 'curtain slot' in front. One column has been restored to its plinth and the dressing rooms for the actors are to the right of the stage. Excavation of the site revealed striking evidence of the decline of the Roman civilization. In the fourth century the theatre became a refuse dump for the nearby market hall.

37 Roman Temple, Weycock Hill, Berkshire

Before the adoption of Christianity the Romans worshipped a variety of different gods. This temple was discovered and excavated in 1847. It is in the shape of a double octagon 19.5m (64ft) across with walls 1.1m (3½ft) thick which were built with mortared flints. After the excavation the location of the site was lost until rediscovered in recent years through aerial photography. Traces can also be seen of the surrounding rectangular enclosure or 'Temenos'.

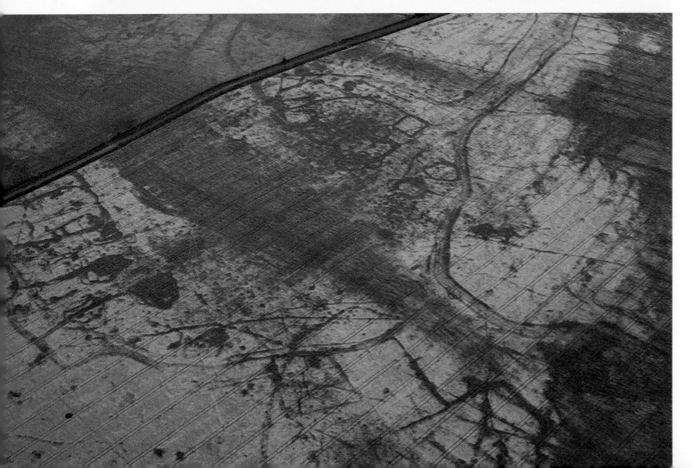

38 Romano-British Settlement, Cote, Oxfordshire

This Romano-British settlement is showing up as a cropmark in a field of ripening barley. It consists of huts and rectangular enclosures grouped together in an oval layout. The many small dots are food-storage pits, and trackways can also be seen leading into the settlement.

39 Roman Road, Berkshire

Roman roads were usually laid out in straight lines between prominent points, often several miles apart. Deviations from the straight, where they occur, are usually due to natural obstacles encountered by the road engineers, as the overriding requirement was the shortest possible route. Some roads followed earlier trackways, just as modern roads occasionally follow the route of a Roman road. This photograph shows part of a Roman road from Silchester to London which is still a trackway. Unspoilt by modern development, it is known as the 'Devil's Highway' and is revealed as a straight line of trees and hedges following field boundaries in the East Berkshire countryside.

40 Housteads Roman Fort, Northumberland

Housteads was one of the major forts on Hadrian's Wall, about half-way along it. It measures 186m x 112m (610ft x 367ft). The garrison at Housteads was a military cohort (800 men). This photograph, taken just before sunset, highlights the buildings inside the fort. In the centre are the headquarters buildings; above them are the granaries, whilst the long rectangular buildings are the barracks which provided accommodation for the Roman soldiers.

RIGHT

41 Portchester Castle, Hampshire

This large, square fort is among the most notable remains of Roman Britain. It dates from the end of the third century AD and was one of a series of forts constructed to defend the southeast coast of Britain against continuing waves of Saxon invaders. These forts are commonly known as the 'Roman Forts of the Saxon Shore'. Portchester stands on the edge of an inlet in Portsmouth Harbour. Within its 3.6 hectares (9 acres) are the inner bailey and keep of a medieval castle constructed during the reign of Henry II (1154–89) and the chapel of an Augustinian Priory founded in 1133, which is now a parish church. Until 1964 little was known about the internal area of the fort but in that year traces of a military timber building, probably a barrack block, were excavated together with the remains of a cobbled road leading to one of the gateways. Saxon pottery found during the excavation would tend to confirm the landing of the Saxons in the region of Portsmouth in 501 AD as mentioned in the *Anglo-Saxon Chronicle*.

42 Pevensey Castle, Sussex

Pevensey has a long and stirring history. Here the Romans built their great fortress Anderida, which formed part of the Saxon shore defences. When it was constructed Pevensey Castle was situated at the end of a peninsula. Unlike its contemporaries it is oval in plan. The walls probably followed the contours of the land raised above the level of the sea and the surrounding marshes. Now the sea has receded and Pevensey is some distance inland. The wall, made from Roman concrete, was faced with stonework and is supported at intervals by bastions which also provided defensive positions. The fort was overrun by the Saxons in 961 AD. In 1066 William the Conqueror landed at Pevensey before advancing to attack King Harold's army on the Senlac plain, near what is now Battle. The military value of Pevensey was recognized after the Norman Conquest and the fort was strengthened by Robert, Count of Mortain. A keep was built in the south-east corner and a smaller inner bailey was fortified within the Roman walls. Alterations were made to the castle in the thirteenth century when the curtain walls, with their round-fronted towers, replaced the original timber palisade. The castle was further fortified during the threat of the Spanish Armada in 1587–88 and again during the Second World War, in 1940.

43 Richborough Castle, Kent

Richborough is one of the most important monuments of Roman Britain. It was here that the Roman Legions assembled after landing in Britain during the Claudian invasion of 43 AD. Some 40 years later a large monument was erected in the centre of the site to commemorate the event. The cruciform foundation we see here is believed to be the base of this monument. The triple ditch surrounding it is the remains of a third-century fort. In the near left-hand corner of the fort are the foundations of a second-century house which was partly destroyed when the triple ditches were dug. The stone-and-concrete walls of the Saxon shore fort which is rectangular in plan were erected in the later part of the third century AD.

44 Reculver Fort, Kent

Situated on the south bank of the Thames estuary, about one third of Reculver has been destroyed by coastal erosion. In the centre of the fort are the ruins of a church founded in about 669 AD by Egbert, King of Kent. Reculver was the first of the Roman shore forts to be constructed.

BELOW LEFT

45 The Wansdyke, Wiltshire

With the coming of the Saxons, a series of boundaries were set up. Running across the Wiltshire countryside, the Wansdyke is one of the finest linear earthworks in Britain, and was once thought to be the boundary of Wessex, the kingdom of the West Saxons. Excavations now indicate that it belongs to the early part of the 'Dark Ages' and was probably built in the period immediately after the decline of Roman Britain as a defence against the earliest Saxon invaders.

RIGHT

46 Bosham, Sussex

A fishing village in Chichester harbour, Bosham has its origins in the Saxon period. The church in the centre of the photograph features on the Bayeux Tapestry. It was here that King Canute is alleged to have tried to turn back the encroaching tide. His daughter is buried in the church.

52

47 Hastings Castle, Sussex

The castle was possibly founded by William the Conqueror soon after the Battle of Hastings (which took place further inland). Its construction is depicted in the Bayeux Tapestry. The only trace of William's castle that remains is a slight mound. The stone walls are later in date. The castle is built in a commanding position on a high clifftop overlooking the English Channel. The first tournament ever held in Britain is supposed to have been staged here in the presence of King John.

48 Wallingford Castle, Oxfordshire

After the Battle of Hastings, William the Conqueror marched on London. He met no opposition until he attempted to cross London Bridge. Driven back by the citizens of Saxon London, he followed the south bank of the River Thames to the first place where the river could be forded – Wallingford. Marking an important river crossing, the castle at Wallingford was one of the first 'motte-and-bailey' castles to be built by William. The mound or motte can be seen on the right of the picture and the bailey is still clearly visible from the air. At ground level the castle is less distinct. The castle was completed in 1071 AD. A town grew up around the castle but was ravaged by the plague in 1349 after which only 44 houses remained. In recent years the local residents successfully campaigned against the castle site's becoming a building development.

49 Berkhamsted Castle, Hertfordshire

In appearance this is a typical early Norman castle and was far removed from the stately edifice of stone which many associate with the very word 'castle'. It was based on one of the earliest methods of fortification – an earthwork. Except for a few rare instances the early Norman castle was devoid of any stone construction. An important feature was a mound or 'motte' flattened at the top, on which a circular wooden keep was erected. Below the mound was the 'bailey', a simple enclosure sometimes protected by an earthen rampart and deep ditch with counterscarp. Berkhamsted is a very good example of an early motte-and-bailey castle. Its stone walls were added at a later date.

50 Windsor Castle, Berkshire

Windsor Castle is the largest castle in the world; it is the longest continuously inhabited castle and is still used as a royal residence. William the Conqueror built the original castle around 1070. Although the first castle was almost certainly built of wood, the outline of the Norman motte and bailey is still clearly visible in this view down on the Royal Apartments looking towards the Round Tower. The Round Tower and the outer walls were built of stone during the reign of Henry II. In the top of the picture is St George's Chapel, begun by Edward IV but not completed until the reign of Henry VIII (1528). Considerable alterations to the castle were carried out under the direction of Sir Jeffry Wyatville during the reign of George IV, and much of the castle's external appearance today is the result of his work.

56

51 Launceston Castle, Cornwall

In a commanding position overlooking the market town of Launceston is Sir Robert Mortain's castle. Sir Robert came to Britain with William the Conqueror and was rewarded for his efforts by being made Earl of Cornwall. His castle was a simple earthwork structure with a timber keep and palisade. The keep was replaced with a circular stone wall in about 1216 and later a round tower was built within the wall. By the time the keep was constructed changes in military architecture had made it almost obsolete, for the current fashion favoured the fortification of large areas using a curtain wall with several entrances through which besiegers could be counter-attacked. The photograph shows the castle in relation to the town. Within the castle green an archaeological excavation is taking place.

52 Restormel Castle, Cornwall

Built around 1100 by the Norman landowner, Baldwin FitzTurstin, Restormel was probably intended to protect the nearby bridge crossing the River Fowey. The castle is surrounded by a circular, flat-bottomed ditch, the earth having been dug out to provide the mound on which the stone keep was constructed. The internal structure of the castle consists of a circular courtyard surrounded by two storeys of buildings. Most of the ground floor was used for storage with accommodation above. An interesting feature of the castle is a vertical speaking-tube built into the wall – a medieval sort of intercom. Restormel was held for Parliament against the Royalists in the Civil War. Sir Richard Grenville laid siege to it and captured it within a few days. The castle was never used again.

54 Rochester Castle, Kent

Here is an unusual combination of castle and cathedral almost side by side. What makes Rochester so imposing is one of the highest Norman keeps in England. The keep was constructed around 1127 when Henry I gave the castle to William de Corbeil, Archbishop of Canterbury. The keep is 21m (70ft) square and rises to a total height of 38m (125ft). On the right of the picture is Rochester Cathedral. It was begun in 1077 on the site of an earlier church founded by St Augustine in 604 AD. Destroyed by fire in 1137 and 1179, it was again rebuilt in the mid-twelfth century. In 1201, a baker named William from Perth, who was known for his generosity towards the poor, spent the night here and was murdered on a nearby road the next day. He was buried in the cathedral and soon afterwards miracles are said to have occurred at his tomb. The cathedral had its own martyr's shrine, which became a centre for pilgrimage. By the thirteenth century, funds were sufficient for the east end to be rebuilt. The building originally formed part of a monastery and after the dissolution by Henry VIII in 1540, it was reconstituted as a Protestant Cathedral.

53 Dover Castle, Kent

Dover was an important site long before the castle was constructed. The hilltop was once an Iron Age fortress. Within this fort the Romans built a lighthouse in the first century AD. The Saxons constructed a church on the site nearly 1000 years later. The Normans built the castle which, with later additions, remained active until the seventeenth century. The most im-pressive part is the huge square keep built soon after 1180 by Henry II. The reason for the choice of site is easy to appreciate: the natural strength of the hilltop position combined with the harbour below the cliff which opens onto the shortest passage to the continent of Europe. Dover is one of the most impressive medieval fortresses in Europe.

55 The Tower of London

London's castle is one of the most historic fortresses in Europe. It was founded by William the Conqueror to protect London from the eastern sea approach soon after the Norman invasion of 1066. The main keep or 'White Tower' dates from his reign. It is largely unaltered despite medieval additions and windows added by Sir Christopher Wren. Although largely built of white stone imported from Caen in France, it owes its name to Henry III who had it whitewashed both inside and out. Successive Kings of England have added to its fortifications. It has served as a palace and a prison and held many illustrious captives, most of whom escaped only by way of the executioner's block. In this photograph from the River Thames, its overall layout can readily be grasped.

56 Bamburgh Castle, Northumberland

A restored Norman castle, this stands in a dramatic setting on the Northumberland coast. The site is thought to have first been fortified by the Anglian King Ida the Flamebearer in 547 AD. Bamburgh is built on a site which is itself elevated, making the construction of a motte unnecessary. The castle has a fine example of a square keep dating from the period of Henry II. Although the castle was considered impregnable it was captured in 1464 by the Earl of Warwick using two large cannons.

57 Corfe Castle, Dorset

In a commanding position overlooking the gap in the Purbeck Hills, the site was fortified during the Saxon period and it was here that the Saxon King Edward was murdered in 978 AD. William the Conqueror utilized and enlarged the existing Saxon earthworks. The castle was altered during the early twelfth century when the tall keep and inner bailey were constructed, and again during the reign of King Edward II in 1300. It was eventually destroyed by the Parliamentary forces during the Civil War in 1646. This view shows the castle from the south.

seen silhouetted in the courtyard (left). The castle was captured after a siege during the Civil War in 1646, plundered of its contents, then mined with explosives and burned. It was used as a quarry for building stone until the eighteenth century, but enough remains for the strength and design of the castle to be appreciated.

RIGHT
59 Pembroke Castle, Dyfed, South Wales

After the Norman invasion of England a native Welsh prince, Rhys ap Tewdwr, succeeded in gaining William I's recognition as a vassal. This was a shrewd move for it kept the Normans out of the area for some years. But his death in battle in 1093 opened the floodgates and the Normans swept in taking most of the Welsh by surprise. The Norman successes were consolidated by a series of castles built at strategic points. At first a timber castle was established at Pembroke, but this was replaced by the present castle soon after 1207, by William Marshal, Earl of Pembroke. It was substantially complete by the end of the century. The strong circular keep 23 metres (75ft) high and walls 6 metres (19ft) thick at the base represented a significant development in castle design and are ringed by a turreted curtain wall. Pembroke became an important base for the Norman invasions of Ireland, and was the birthplace of Henry Tudor, later to become Henry VII. It was never captured by the Welsh and withstood a seven-week siege from Cromwell's forces, only surrendering through lack of water. Beyond the castle is the town which developed within the protection of a wall, only fragments of which survive. The settlement was divided up into a series of regular linear plots which can clearly be seen from the air. Though typical of some medieval towns this layout is rare within a walled town where land was at a premium.

58 Raglan Castle, Gwent, South Wales

Raglan Castle is thought to have been built on the site of an earlier fortified structure, although there was little trace of this remaining when Sir William ap Thomas began the construction of the present castle around 1430. The Great Tower, which is hexagonal in plan, dates from this period, and can be seen at the top of the picture. With walls over 3m (10ft) thick and surrounded by a water-filled moat, it was a fortress in its own right separated from the rest of the castle by a drawbridge. During a period of uncertainty, this provided the owner with protection against the possible unreliability of his own soldiers. Sir William died in 1445 and the castle was largely completed by his son, Sir William Herbert, Earl of Pembroke. The residential quarters were improved and extended during the sixteenth century, and large Elizabethan windows in the great hall can be

1958; behind that is Thomas Telford's elegant suspension bridge, completed in 1826, with towers to match those of the castle. In 1848 the engineer Robert Stephenson built a tubular railway bridge with castellated towers to carry the railway over the Conway River *en route* to Holyhead.

RIGHT

61 Tenby, Dyfed, South Wales

Tenby is the finest example of a medieval fortified town in South Wales. Its town wall, which is well preserved, can be seen in the foreground. It was built in the late thirteenth century to protect the citizens of the town after it had been sacked twice, in 1187 and again in 1260. Along the length of the wall, half-round towers were built at intervals of 15–30 metres (50–100ft), which enabled each tower to give covering fire to its neighbour. A castle was built on the peninsula (top of picture) in about 1153. Little of it remains today although the site was one of great natural strength, being a steep-sided promontory, joined to the coast by a narrow neck of land. During the Civil War the castle took part in a rather unusual battle – a cannon duel with Parliamentary ships lying offshore. To the right of the peninsula is St Catherine's Island surmounted by a fort built in the 1860s as part of the South Coast defences against the French. The houses around the harbour are not small fishermen's cottages but elegant Georgian houses, a relic of the prosperous merchant community that traded between here and Ireland. The advent of the railway combined with the shallowness of the harbour killed off the sea trade, but in its place the tourist industry has thrived.

60 Conway, Gwynedd, North Wales

Conway was built by Edward I as part of his plan to subdue North Wales, and was both fortress and garrison town. It is one of the most perfect examples surviving in Europe of a planned medieval town, being surrounded by a wall almost 1.2km (¾ mile) in length with 22 towers spaced along it at regular intervals and three original gateways. The castle, sited in the southern corner of the town, is undoubtedly one of the finest in Wales. The walls and the castle were built rapidly between 1283 and 1287 at a cost of £15,000 (equivalent to over ten million pounds at today's prices). Three bridges span the river to the left of the castle. In the foreground is a modern road bridge built in

62 Farnham Castle, Surrey

The castle originally had a square tower, built in 1138. This was enclosed by an earthwork on which the present curtain wall stands. In the late twelfth century the tower was demolished and replaced by the masonry of the present keep. This is a rare example of construction whereby the shell wall, instead of being built around the summit of the motte is built around its base and then carried up as a revetment to the whole mound. Most of the surrounding domestic buildings were added at this time or early in the thirteenth century. Its appearance was again altered during the fifteenth century by the addition of a large brick gatehouse. The castle was the residence of the Bishops of Winchester from the time of its construction until 1927.

63 Nunney Castle, Somerset

During the fourteenth century, castle construction underwent a change as conditions in Britain became more stable. Not so much a fortress, the castle was more a place to live in (although this had always been a major part of its role). During periodic threats of invasion from Europe the owners of manor houses in some areas were granted a licence to fortify or 'crenellate' their houses. Licences were often liberally interpreted and often the houses ended up resembling a medieval fortress. Nunney is one such example. It was completed in 1373 after Sir John de la Mare obtained a licence to crenellate his house. Rectangular, with a round tower at each corner, it was a compact and well-fortified manor surrounded by a moat. It was attacked by Oliver Cromwell's forces using cannon during the Civil War in 1645 and then became a ruin.

64 Bodiam Castle, Sussex

The nearby towns of Rye and Winchelsea had been attacked and burned by the French when Richard II granted one of his knights, Sir Edward Dalyngrigge, a licence to strengthen his manor house in 1385. Sir Edward interpreted the licence very loosely and on a new site nearby built one of the last medieval castles in Britain. It was built at a time when considerations of comfort were beginning to weigh equally with defence in castle planning. The symmetrical plan of the courtyard castle and its large rectangular moat can clearly be seen in this aerial view.

65 Hever Castle, Kent

Hever is really a fortified manor house. The licence to strengthen its defences was granted in about 1340. Exactly what work was done then is uncertain but the fresh threat of French invasion inspired further work around 1384. The quadrangular house and moat date from this time. The three-storey gatehouse was built around 1462. The extensive landscaping and the 'Tudor Village' behind the main house were not completed until the early part of this century. It was here that Henry VIII courted his second wife, Anne Boleyn. He later acquired Hever and gave it to his fourth wife, Anne of Cleves. It then passed through several families until by the nineteenth century it was a working farmhouse. It was extensively restored at the beginning of the present century.

66 Leeds Castle, Kent

Leeds has one of the most beautiful settings of any English castle. It is situated on two islands in the middle of an artificial lake formed in the fourteenth century by flooding the River Len. The stone castle dates from the twelfth century but has been considerably altered over the years. Richard II commissioned Henry Yevele to carry out improvements at Leeds and later Henry VIII spent a considerable sum transforming it from a fortress into a palace, although he retained the castle's defences. He was the last royal owner. The castle was again altered and 'medievalized' in the nineteenth century.

RIGHT
67 Warwick Castle, Warwickshire

Warwick Castle is one of the few great medieval fortresses in England which are still inhabited and is particularly striking when seen from the air. It was once the seat of the Earls of Warwick and was started in the eleventh century, although much of what can be seen today, including the curtain wall and massive tower defence system, dates from the fourteenth century. Additional building was carried out in the seventeenth and eighteenth centuries, mainly on the domestic side of the castle.

should live at Battle, he began to extend the house but died before it was finished. The house has been lived in ever since but was extensively restored in 1933 after it had been gutted by fire. This view shows the abbey ruins from the south with the medieval town of Battle in the background.

69 Canterbury Cathedral, Kent

Canterbury Cathedral dates back to the days of St Augustine, the Roman missionary, who converted Ethelbert, King of Kent. Ever since the arrival of St Augustine's mission in 597 AD, Canterbury has been the focal point of the Church of England and seat of the primate Archbishop. The oldest remaining parts of the cathedral date from Archbishop Lanfranc of Bec (1070–1089). Although little of his work is visible, the ground plan of his cathedral was largely adhered to during subsequent rebuilding operations. The murder of Thomas à Becket in 1170 by four of Henry II's knights resulted in the building's becoming one of the most celebrated centres for pilgrimages in Britain. The subsequent increase in funds enabled considerable building work to take place. Most of the structure is the work of later builders, notably William of Sens, a French mason, who began work in 1175. The main central tower known as 'Bell Harry' was designed by William Westall in the late fifteenth century. Apart from the north-west tower, built to replace an earlier one which collapsed in 1832, the cathedral has been little altered and is much as it was at the time of the dissolution in the sixteenth century. One of the most interesting tombs in the cathedral is that of the 'Black Prince', Edward, Prince of Wales (1330–76), who defeated the French and captured their king at Poitiers in 1356. This view shows Canterbury from the south-west.

68 Battle Abbey, Sussex

According to the *Anglo-Saxon Chronicle*, Battle Abbey was built by William I on 'the spot where God allowed him to conquer England'. Contemporary sources attribute the abbey to William Faber, a monk of Marmoutier who had been in the service of the King. He built the abbey some distance from the spot because of unstable ground conditions and so as to be nearer a source of water. In 1338 the abbey was fortified and the gatehouse constructed. Like many abbeys it was dissolved by Henry VIII and the last abbot surrendered it in 1538. The King granted the house and abbey remains to his Master of the Horse Sir Anthony Browne. On the death of the King, Sir Anthony was one of the executors of his will, and Princess Elizabeth was under his care. With the idea that she

73

70 Old Sarum, Wiltshire

This is the site of the original town of Salisbury. It was built within the vast circular earthen ramparts of an Iron Age hillfort. In the centre of the site surrounded by a moat are the remains of a castle and to the left of this are the foundations of the cathedral which was completed by Bishop St Osmund (1078–99). The crowding together of castle, cathedral and city in such a confined space coupled with a lack of water eventually led to the abandonment of the town and the founding of the new town of Salisbury in the valley to the south.

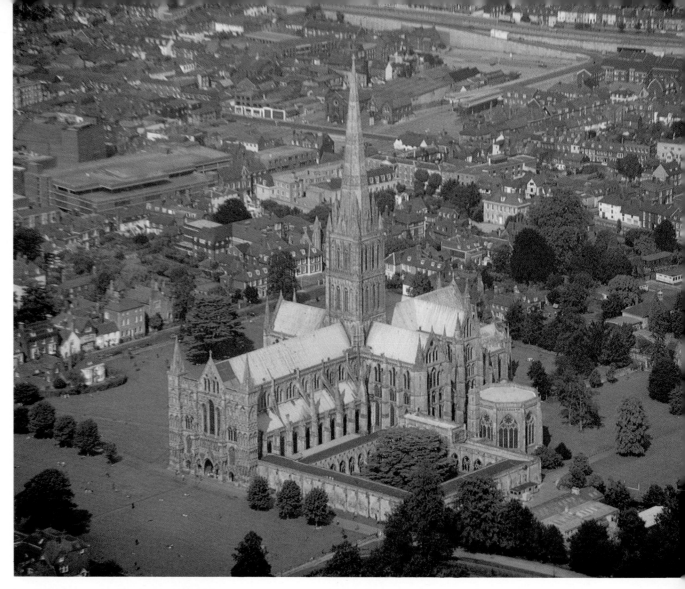

71 Salisbury Cathedral, Wiltshire

Dominating the town of Salisbury and a landmark for many miles around, Salisbury Cathedral was begun in 1220 and substantially completed in less than 40 years. The spire was added later in 1320. It is 124m (406ft) high and made Salisbury Cathedral the tallest structure in Britain until the erection of Blackpool Tower in 1895. Edward III licensed the Dean and Chapter to demolish the earlier cathedral at Old Sarum and much of the stone was used in the fabric of the new cathedral and its precincts.

75

72 Durham Cathedral, Durham

Prominent among Celtic missionaries was St Cuthbert who from Lindisfarne, the holy island off the Northumberland coast, did much to spread Christianity across northern England. He died and was buried in 687 AD, but with the growing terror of the Danish and Norse raids it became necessary to exhume his remains and take them to more secure surroundings. Thus the Lindisfarne brotherhood set out on a re- markable pilgrimage of 120 years' duration. In 997 AD the brothers arrived with his body at 'Dunholme'. Attracted by the security of the hill, surrounded on three sides by the River Wear, they built a church on the site where Durham Cathedral now stands. The dramatic setting emphasizing the security of the position is clearly illustrated in this aerial view. Such was the origin of one of the most outstanding examples of Romanesque architecture in Europe: the Norman cathedral was begun in 1093 by Bishop William of Calais and is notable for its stone carvings. Behind the cathedral can be seen Durham Castle, the earliest phases dating from about 1070. Considerable restora- tion of the castle took place in the nineteenth century.

73 Winchester Cathedral, Hampshire

Winchester is a town important in England's history and was, for a considerable period, the capital. A Celtic stronghold, it became the Roman town of Venta Belgarum. At the begin- ning of the Saxon invasion, Winchester was probably only held as a fort, but when Cedric founded the Kingdom of Wessex in about 519, Winchester was chosen as the capital. In 634 the missionary Birinus and his followers landed on the Hampshire coast and converted King Cyne- gils to the Christian faith. Winchester then became an important centre for Christian teaching. The present cathedral is the second largest in Europe and its cruciform shape can readily be appreciated in this photograph. Dedi- cated to St Swithun (known in folklore for his rainmaking ability), it was begun in 1079 by Walkelin, the first Norman bishop, who was a relative of William the Conquerer, and com- pleted by Bishop Henry of Blois in 1170. The cathedral was built on the site of an earlier Saxon church in which Edward the Confessor was crowned in 1043. The external appearance, although comparatively simple, is of great architectural value, for it is representative of all the successive styles from the eleventh to the sixteenth century. In 1905, the eleventh century foundation had begun to weaken and the south and east sides of the cathedral would have collapsed, but for the efforts of a diver, William Walker, who worked for six years in complete darkness in shafts up to 6 metres deep under- neath the walls, rebuilding the foundations in bricks and cement. Among the notable people buried in the Cathedral are Egbert, the first king of all England, Canute, and William II (Rufus) who was killed in a hunting accident in the nearby New Forest. Mary I was married to Philip of Spain here in 1554.

74 York Minster, Yorkshire

York Minster is the largest Gothic church in England and ranges in style from Early English to Perpendicular. It had humble beginnings as a small wooden church where Paulinus, first Bishop of York, baptized Edwin, the Northumbrian King in 627 AD, an event described by the Venerable Bede, who in one of his most famous passages compares the life of man to a sparrow, flying through a lighted hall, in one door and out of the other. Since that time there has been a succession of Saxon and Norman churches at York. The present church was begun by Archbishop Walter de Grey in 1227, and the massive central tower, which is the largest in England, dates from the fifteenth century. In this view from the south-west, the cathedral can be seen in relation to the medieval city of York in the foreground. The narrow streets, known as the 'Shambles', contain many antique and souvenir shops catering for the large tourist industry that has built up in recent years.

75 St Albans Abbey, Hertfordshire

This cathedral is said to have been founded on the spot where St Alban was martyred. A Roman living in the nearby town of Verulamium, Alban gave shelter to a Christian fleeing persecution, which resulted in his execution. The present building dates from 1077 although the abbey is thought to have been founded by King Offa II of Mercia in the eighth century AD. The Norman church was almost entirely built using bricks salvaged from the Roman town close by. The abbey was dissolved by Henry VIII in 1539 and the abbey church was taken over and used as the parish church of the town. In the early nineteenth century part of a wall collapsed and urgent repairs were carried out. At the end of the nineteenth century when the church was again in a state of disrepair Lord Grimthorpe carried out extensive restoration work at an expenditure of £250,000. Much of the exterior appearance of the building is due to his work, carried out in a Victorian Gothic style. It became a cathedral in 1877 and is the second longest in England.

parish church. The wall of the nave remains as the Normans built it and the buttresses on the walls date from the fourteenth century. In the churchyard is a fourteenth-century gabled building which was the village school in the seventeenth century and now houses Dorchester Museum. This is a view towards the abbey church from the south-west, with part of the medieval town of Dorchester in the foreground.

77 Whitby Abbey, Yorkshire
Whitby is a fishing port on the North Yorkshire coast whose history goes back to 664 AD, when the Council of Whitby did much to establish Christianity in this part of Britain. The Saxon Abbess, Hilda, built an abbey here which was sacked by the Danes in 867 AD. On the clifftop in the left of the picture are the ruins of the Benedictine monastery founded in 1078. Originally a priory, Whitby became an abbey in the early twelfth century, and was soon one of the wealthiest in Yorkshire. The abbey and town were plundered in 1153 by King Eystein Haroldson of Norway, and in the thirteenth century the church was rebuilt. The abbey was dissolved in 1539 and the timber roof and bells were removed immediately. The church structure was left intact, probably because it was a landmark for local mariners. Between 1762 and 1794 most of the nave fell, followed by the south transept and much of the west front.

76 Dorchester, Oxfordshire
Dorchester was the Roman town of Dorocina, an important settlement on the Roman road from Silchester to Alchester. According to Bede, in 635 AD Birinus, the missionary to the West Saxons, baptized the Saxon King Cynegils in the nearby River Thames. Soon afterwards he built a cathedral which remained a stronghold of Christianity in the area until Winchester succeeded Dorchester as the seat of the Bishops. The present church is the only remaining part of an Augustinian abbey, founded on the site of the cathedral in 1170; it flourished until dissolved by Henry VIII. The abbey church was purchased from Henry's commissioners for £140 by Richard Beaulieu who gave it for a

78 Glastonbury Abbey, Somerset

Glastonbury Abbey is the legendary burial site of King Arthur. In 1191 the monks claimed to have discovered his tomb and that of his queen, Guinevere. The royal couple were reburied in April 1278 in the presence of King Edward I in a black marble tomb which survived on the site until the dissolution of the abbey in 1539. It is clear that Glastonbury was a sacred site before the Normans built the first abbey, destroyed by fire in 1184. The destruction was so complete that none of the standing walls is any earlier than this date. It is likely that Glastonbury was once a pagan sanctuary which would explain the coming of some of the earliest missionaries to the area. The abbey church at the top of the picture was completed in its first phase by Christmas Day 1213 and the nave and west end were added before 1250. The small square building in the foreground with its roughly conical roof is the abbot's house – here the abbot entertained visitors. The abbot's kitchen, dating from the fourteenth century, is one of the most complete medieval kitchens to survive in Europe.

79 Oronsay Priory, Inner Hebrides, Scotland

Oronsay is a small island to the south of Colonsay. It is separated from it by a shallow channel which can be forded at low tide. St Columba is thought to have landed here in 563 AD but because he could still see his native Ireland, he moved north to Iona. Later an Augustinian priory was built on the site. Its foundation is obscure, but it has been attributed to John of Islay around 1360. The roofless church is 18m (60ft) long and together with the adjoining cloister it is simple and undecorated. Close to the wall in the centre of the picture is a large cross decorated with a relief of the crucifixion, dated 1510. In the grounds are many sixteenth-century tomb slabs. The priory was often used as a sanctuary for people fleeing justice and an eroded cross marks the boundary within which fugitives had to remain for a year and a day.

80 Tintern Abbey, Gwent, South Wales

Beautifully situated in the valley of the River Wye and surrounded by wooded hills, Tintern is one of the most romantic ruins in Britain. Founded in 1131, it was not completed until one-and-a-half centuries later. Apart from the roof and the north aisle arcade in the nave, the main fabric of the church stands almost complete. Tintern exhibits simple Cistercian architecture and has no large towers, as these were forbidden by the Cistercian order. Cistercian ruins are generally more extensive than those of other orders because it was their custom to build in the countryside, whilst the Benedictines, for example, chose places that were already inhabited. Thus, after the dissolution, ruins forming parts of towns were pulled down to be replaced by churches, or incorporated into wooden houses. In open country however the sites were of less value and the abbey buildings were left to decay at the mercy only of local road builders and farmers, who looked upon them as valuable quarries. In this view looking at Tintern from the north, some of the foundations of the monastic buildings can be seen in the foreground. The square to the left of the north transept is the infirmary cloister, with the abbot's hall below this and the infirmary hall to the left. The abbey was dissolved in 1536 and the site and buildings given to Henry Somerset, Earl of Worcester. The buildings were then systematically stripped of their roofs for lead.

81 Quarr Abbey, Isle of Wight

The original abbey at Quarr was founded in 1132 and like so many others was dissolved by Henry VIII in 1536, the remains being used as farm buildings. For nearly 400 years monastic life at Quarr was little more than a memory until 1907 when the French Benedictine monks of Solesmes, who were forced to leave their own country because of anti-monastic laws, took refuge in the Isle of Wight. They bought Quarr Abbey House which was partly built using stone from the earlier abbey. This formed the nucleus for the new monastery which was completed in 1908. The church was added in 1911–12. Built of Flemish brick, it is a particularly fine example of the architecture of that period.

82 St Michael's Mount, Cornwall

This rocky, granite island off the south-west coast of Cornwall is thought to be Ictis from where the Mediterranean traders bartered for tin in the first century BC. The Benedictine Priory of St Michael's Mount was built by Bernard Le Bec, Abbot of Mont St Michel, a similar island surmounted by an abbey off the Breton coast of France. It became an important centre for pilgrimage until the church fell in a severe earthquake. Most of the present buildings date from the twelfth century but the Chapel of St Michael with its battlemented tower was not constructed until the fifteenth. In 1587 a beacon on top of the church tower signalled the approach of the Spanish Armada. The monastery was transformed into a mansion after 1659, and the south-east wing, in the style of a Gothic castle, added in 1873. St Michael's Mount was given to the National Trust in 1954.

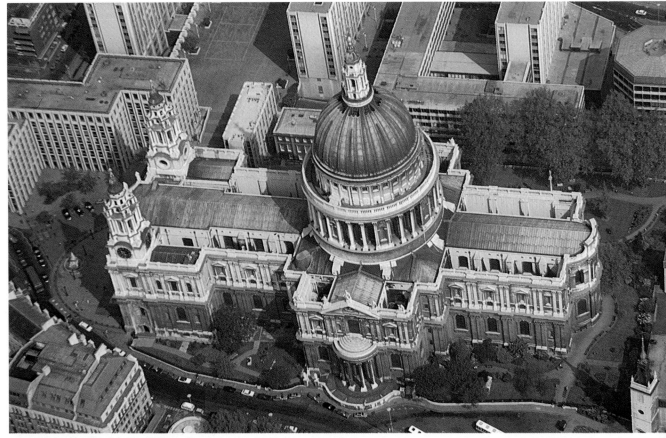

83 St Paul's Cathedral, London

One of London's most distinctive buildings, St Paul's Cathedral was designed by Sir Christopher Wren to replace the earlier Gothic cathedral destroyed by the Great Fire of London in 1666. Wren's design was his third attempt and is a compromise between his insistence on a Classical cathedral with a dome and the clergy's preference for a cruciform plan. The foundation stone was laid without any formal ceremony in 1675. The dome is the second largest in the world and is estimated to weigh about 65 million kilogrammes. St Paul's has been used for many famous Royal and State events. An unusual feature is the outer wall complete with its false windows, designed to conceal the buttress supports which can clearly be seen from above. The construction of the cathedral was largely funded by a tax on coal brought into the port of London. Wren is buried within the Cathedral and his Latin epitaph can be translated as, 'If you would seek his monument, look around you'.

84a & b Liverpool's Two Cathedrals, Merseyside

Liverpool's two cathedrals, one Anglican, the other Roman Catholic, are both comparatively recent creations. The Anglican cathedral is built in a somewhat traditional Gothic style, and is the second largest cathedral in the world. It was designed by Sir Giles Gilbert Scott in 1901. Construction began in 1904 but the two World Wars and a shortage of funds delayed its completion until the early 1970s. An unusual feature of the cathedral is that it is set north-south instead of the conventional east-west. This was dictated by the line of the limestone ridge on which the building is founded. It is probably one of the last cathedrals in Britain that will ever be built from stone – a local pink sandstone was used. Rising costs have made this form of construction impracticable. By contrast the tent-shaped structure of the Roman Catholic cathedral is an example of modern architecture. It is made of reinforced concrete and was built in a period of only four years. Frederick Gibberd was the architect and it was completed in 1967. The plan reflects modern liturgical thought with its emphasis on audience participation, rather than having an altar at the end of the building; it can claim the distinction of having a car park under the nave!

RIGHT ABOVE
85 Stoke Poges Church, Buckinghamshire

The Norman church of Stoke Poges is set in the quiet countryside only a few minutes' walk from the bustle of the Slough Industrial Estate. The church is the product of several periods of building dating from about 1086 up to 1558. Its main claim to fame is that in 1750, under the yew tree opposite the south-west door of the church, the poet Thomas Gray is said to have written his 'Elegy written in a Country Churchyard'. The tree is in the bottom left-hand corner of the picture. Thomas Gray died on 6 August 1771. He was buried in the nearer of the two large tombs that can be seen close to the east wall of the church.

RIGHT BELOW
86 Eythrope, Near Aylesbury, Buckinghamshire: Deserted Medieval Village

It is thought that there are as many as two thousand deserted medieval villages in England. They were abandoned for a variety of reasons. The Black Death of 1348–9 is often quoted as the main cause but it probably only contributed to an already deteriorating situation. During the fourteenth century the weather became much wetter; harvests failed and much land under cultivation was abandoned as unworkable. Also landowners tempted by the high price of wool began to lay large areas of arable land down to grass. Where many men had laboured only a few shepherds were needed to tend the flocks. Later, during the seventeenth and eighteenth centuries, villages were removed by some of the great landowners who wished them further away from their residences. Many deserted villages have never been under the plough but remained as rough pasture. Their outline is often revealed by shadows cast just before sunset. In this photograph the trackway can be seen leading into the village through the ridge and furrow field systems. The village is contained within the curved boundary where the street system and house platforms are clearly visible.

87 Deserted Medieval Village, Waldridge, Buckinghamshire

The village, about five miles south-west of Aylesbury, is revealed here by the pattern of melting snow which is lying thicker over the street system; the plan of the village stands out clearly in this aerial photograph. The cultivation pattern of the surrounding fields can also clearly be seen.

RIGHT

88 Ridge-and-Furrow Cultivation System, Buckinghamshire

The ridge-and-furrow field system formed the basis for the layout of many later medieval towns and villages. The 'furlongs' varied in size on account of natural factors. The strips represent the work of families who cleared the 'furlong' and are not always straight. A typical size is ¼–⅓ acre (0.10–0.13 hectare), mostly around 220yd × 5½yd (201m × 5.03m). The strips show up in certain parts of the country where former arable land is now pasture. In the damper climatic conditions which then prevailed, the medieval strain of wheat was prone to mould growth on the stem. This system of cultivation enabled it to be grown on the ridge and irrigated in the furrow.

90

92

89 Hungerford, Berkshire

A view looking south down the main street of the medieval market town of Hungerford. The position of the houses alongside the road together with their long gardens shows that the burgage plots were laid out on the line of the strips of the open fields from an earlier settlement. The original village is thought to have dated from the twelfth century; most of the surviving buildings date from the eighteenth, although a few timber-frame houses survive from the sixteenth and seventeenth centuries. A number of the towns and villages of Britain owe their layout to similar origins.

90 Culham, Oxfordshire

Some English villages have shrunk, for example Culham. In the bottom right-hand corner of the photograph are the manor house and the church, but the cropmarks between these buildings and the bend in the River Thames reveal that the village was once much larger. The lines of field boundaries, streets and trackways can clearly be seen showing up in the crop of ripening barley. The reasons for the decline in the size of the village are similar to those which brought about the desertion of many others (see Plate 86).

91 Mevagissey, Cornwall

Within living memory Mevagissey was an important fishing port. Small white and coloured houses cluster around its picturesque harbour which today is notable for the absence of fishing boats, now replaced by pleasure craft. In the eighteenth century this port was the centre of the pilchard fishing industry. Every year some 35 million pilchards were sent from Mevagissey to Italy alone. There was a harbour pier here in the sixteenth century which was rebuilt in 1775. In 1866 the outer pier was built, increasing the mooring capacity and creating a low-tide harbour, as vessels could not sail into the inner harbour at low tide. In 1850 there were 80 large luggers here, manned by about 300 men. Several factors including ecological changes have since brought about Mevagissey's decline as a fishing port. There is still a small fishing industry here but most of the old offices of the fish merchants down by the harbour are now little 'knick-knack' shops and tourism has taken over as the growth industry. The port has been able to capitalize on its natural beauty and adapt to the change which has saved the port from extinction.

92 Consett, County Durham

Towards the end of 1980 the sun went down for the last time on the operation of the Consett steelworks in Durham. It brought to an end an era of steelmaking and plunged thousands of people out of work, dealing a devastating blow to a community where steelmaking had been their tradition and livelihood for generations. In this picture taken on the very last day of operation the red glow of the setting sun emphasizes the forlorn look of the works and a sense of desolation and quiet already prevails.

96

93 Levant Tin Mine, Botallack, Cornwall

The closing of the Consett steelworks was not a new kind of problem. During the last century the sun set on the last days of operation of much of the Cornish tin-mining industry. This decline was caused in part by falling demand and rising costs – a story similar to that of much industry today. The Levant mine continued working until 1930. In 1919 there was a disaster in the mine when a man-engine, a machine used to bring miners to the surface, failed and 31 men were killed. After this the deeper seams were never worked because the price of tin was at a low level and the mine could not afford the cost of new hoisting gear and other developments. At one stage the mine had been worked to a depth of 610m (2000ft) below sea level. The wheel of fortune has come full circle in recent years, and with increased tin prices and modern mining techniques the tin-mining industry is enjoying something of a revival. Levant is now part of the Geevor mine and one of the more successful mines working in Cornwall.

94 Newcastle-upon-Tyne, Northumberland

This busy industrial town in northern England expanded at a rapid rate during the Industrial Revolution which brought much heavy industry such as shipbuilding to the area. Although the old town is rapidly being engulfed by new development and a complex road system, part of the earlier town which has so far resisted modern change can be seen in the centre of the picture.

95 Liverpool, Merseyside

Liverpool, on the banks of the Mersey, is largely a product of the eighteenth and nineteenth centuries when it developed rapidly from a small fishing village into a port for ships trading with America. In the early part of this century it became a deep-water port for ocean liners. This view shows part of the town's famous water-front. In the centre of the picture, the building with the clock tower is the Royal Liver Building. It was Britain's first 'skyscraper'. Construction began in 1908 and the fifteen floors were completed in just over a year. To the right of this is the Cunard Building and next to it, with the copper dome, is the Mersey Docks and Harbour Board Building. Its elegance reflects an era when the docks were a very profitable undertaking. In the background, almost on the horizon, are the town's two cathedrals. On the right is the Anglican cathedral which is the second-largest cathedral in the world, and on the left the cone-shaped structure is the Roman Catholic cathedral.

RIGHT
96 Bath, Avon

Bath was the Roman 'Aquae Sulis'. The Romans, attracted by the hot springs, built a series of baths and a city grew up around them. Bath was quite a small town when Queen Anne visited it in 1703. A great revival came in the Georgian era when fashionable society was attracted to Bath to take the waters. Developments in the social sphere were accompanied by the remarkable achievement of planning and building what amounted to a new city, seen here to great advantage from the air. The man most responsible for the change was 'Beau Nash'. He encouraged the best architects to transform the town into a 'new Rome', with a series of terraces, crescents and squares which date from around 1730. The principal architects were a father and son both named John Wood. The Royal Crescent on the left of the picture was the work of John Wood the younger. It was built between 1767 and 1775 and consists of 30 houses with great Ionic columns supporting a continuous cornice in the Palladian style. On the right is a circle of houses or 'Circus'. It was the work of John Wood the elder and begun in 1754 but completed by his son. The three tiers of a continuous frieze are supported by columns of the Doric, Ionic and Corinthian orders. Clive of India and the painter Thomas Gainsborough were amongst the notable inhabitants of the Circus. Most of the buildings are made from a golden-brown limestone obtained from quarries at Combe Down to the south of the city.

97 Oxford, Oxfordshire

The Saxons began to settle near the River Thames at Oxford in the fifth century AD, at the point where it could easily be forded by their oxen, hence its name. It was an important centre by the time of King Alfred who set up a mint there in 879 AD. After the Norman Conquest, soon after 1071, Robert d'Oilly built a motte-and-bailey castle in the town to guard the river crossing. Oxford then grew into a busy market town. Why it should have become an important university town no one quite knows. The first college, University College, was founded in 1249. By the time Queen's College was founded in 1340, Oxford University was fully established as a rival to many continental places of learning. The photograph shows part of the centre of Oxford; we can see some of the 'University' buildings, as well as the character-istic layout of 'colleges' at Oxford (and Cambridge) with their quadrangles, dining halls and chapels. The prominent circular building in the middle of the photograph is known as the Radcliffe Camera. It was the first round library in England constructed in 1748 with money left to the university by Dr John Radcliffe, physician to King William III. The green-roofed building to the left of the Radcliffe Camera is the Old Bodleian Library – the second largest library in England with over three million books. The library was despoiled of its books during the Reformation but was revived by Sir Thomas Bodley, Elizabethan diplomat and scholar. Below the Radcliffe Camera is Brasenose College founded in 1509 by William Smyth, Bishop of Lincoln, and Sir William Sutton. In the foreground (centre) is Christ Church. Much of Christ Church was planned and built by Cardinal Wolsey, incorporating the earlier Cathedral (right), which functions also as the college's chapel.

RIGHT

98 Cambridge, Cambridgeshire

As a settlement, Cambridge is probably older than Oxford, although its first college, Peter-house, was not founded until 1284 – nearly 40 years after the first college at Oxford. A settlement existed here in the Iron Age. It later became an important crossing point of the River Cam on the Roman Road from Colchester to Leicester. The Roman settlement established here covered an area of 10 hectares (25 acres). Scholars came from Oxford to Cambridge during the thirteenth century and Henry III declared the town to be a centre of learning. In the centre of the photograph is King's College Chapel. King's College was created by King Henry VI to receive boys from Eton in 1441. For centuries King's remained exclusively a college for Etonians. The chapel was begun in 1446 but not completed until 1515. To the left of the chapel is Clare College, founded in 1326. The large courtyard (top centre-left) with the circular fountain is that of Trinity College, formed by amalgamation of two colleges in 1546. The fountain, added in Elizabethan times, once supplied the college with drinking water. Behind that, the square tower marks St John's College, its fine Tudor building with courtyards bearing a passing resemblance to Hampton Court Palace. Cambridge University is still growing. Its most recent foundation, Robinson's College, dates from 1977.

a

99 a, b, c, d Changing Patterns of Housing

These four photographs reflect changing attitudes in the planning of housing estates and their effect on the townscapes of Britain.

The Industrial Revolution during the nineteenth century had a profound effect on the landscape of Britain. The need to house large numbers of people close to their place of work resulted in the development of high-density housing in the form of cheap back-to-back terrace dwellings. Although it might have provided a short-term solution to the housing problem, it was undoubtedly one of the greatest planning disasters of all time. The houses, laid out in rows, were grim and unhygienic, often lacking basic amenities. By the end of the century, some of the terrace houses were being built with small gardens, which helped to improve the lifestyle of the inhabitants. This can be seen in Plate 99a which shows part of a housing estate in North East London.

By contrast Plate 99b shows part of the Maesgeirchen Housing Estate in North Wales. This estate of some 300 to 350 houses was built in the mid 1930s as part of a re-housing scheme, during a period of slum clearance in the town of

b

Bangor. The houses are all laid out in a circle surrounding a green and have neat gardens.

In the immediate pre-war era the semi-detached house became a popular form of dwelling providing a degree of independence combined with an illusion of privacy. Some interesting patterns emerged as suburban housing estates sprawled out from the cities. Plate 99c is a view of a typical estate of the period in north-west London. After the war, in the 1950s, a fresh wave of building semi-detached houses emerged. Small estates in which houses were grouped around circles or closes helped to foster a feeling of neighbourliness and village life within a town environment.

The 1970s have seen the birth of a number of 'New Towns' planned in small neighbourly groups. Plate 99d shows one of the estates in the New Town of Washington, Tyne and Wear. A mining village was flattened to provide the site and the town was named after an old hall said to have connections with George Washington.

c

d

100 Knole, Kent

Knole, one of the largest private houses in England, is named after the small hill on which it is built. The house is reputed to have 365 rooms, 7 courtyards, and 52 staircases. Originally a medieval house, it was enlarged in 1456 by Thomas Bourchier and converted into a palace for the Archbishops of Canterbury. It was inhabited by successive bishops until Archbishop Cranmer was obliged to hand it over to Henry VIII, who had considerable alterations carried out without, it seems, ever actually living there. Queen Elizabeth I gave it to Thomas Sackville, the first Earl of Dorset, in 1603. Sackville and his son carried out considerable extensions to the house resulting in an expenditure of £40,000 in only ten months. The house has 1.6 hectares (4 acres) of buildings mostly constructed from Kentish ragstone, with irregular roof lines, slender chimney stacks, and battlemented towers. Jacobean gables flank the gateway tower. Bourchier's original gatehouse can be seen behind this tower across the courtyard. The house contains a large collection of Jacobean furniture as well as paintings by Van Dyck and Reynolds. It was given to the National Trust in 1946.

101 Penshurst Place, Kent

This is one of the finest fourteenth-century manor houses to survive in almost its original state, although it has been extended through the centuries, and contains architecture of many periods. It was one of the first country houses to be built for a successful merchant rather than a nobleman. John de Poultney was four times Lord Mayor of London and helped to finance Edward III's Crecy campaigns. Because of a threat of possible attack from France Sir John Devereux was licensed to fortify the house in 1393. Penshurst was the birthplace in 1554 of Sir Philip Sidney, who later became a great soldier and statesman. The terraced formal gardens, which show up well from the air, were begun in 1560 but were largely reconstructed a little over a century ago in the sixteenth-century style. Compare the layout with that of Chatsworth, Plate 104.

in need of modernization. Christopher Wren submitted several schemes – one of them (fortunately not adopted) involved the destruction of all the buildings except the Great Hall. Work on a revised scheme commenced in 1689. Two of the courtyards were unaltered, but the third was demolished to make way for the new Fountain Court, surrounded by a suite of rooms and galleries. Wren used brick with Portland stone embellishments in the classical style. In this aerial view his work can be clearly distinguished from the earlier part of the palace. After the death of George II in 1760 Hampton Court ceased to be occupied by a reigning sovereign. Queen Victoria eventually opened it to the public. The gardens, and in particular the maze are among its most popular attractions.

RIGHT
103 Hatfield House, Hertfordshire
One of England's great houses, Hatfield was the ancestral home of the Cecil family for three-and-a-half centuries. Laid out on a plan characteristic of Elizabethan houses, it is largely the work of the architect Robert Lyminge who began its construction on the site of a former palace in 1607. The centre section is thought by some to be the work of Inigo Jones. The south front as seen in this photograph has not been altered since it was completed for Robert Cecil in 1611. Robert Cecil discovered and suppressed the famous Gunpowder Plot to blow up Parliament and built Hatfield in the hope of attracting royal visits. Unfortunately he died in 1612 just as his new house was nearing completion. The house contains a magnificent Armoury and includes pieces captured from the Spaniards during the Spanish Armada. The landscaped gardens include a maze. Hatfield was one of the first country houses in the last century to have an electric light and telephone system.

102 Hampton Court Palace, Greater London
A former royal palace, Hampton Court was built by Cardinal Wolsey on land leased from the Order of St John of Jerusalem in 1514. Soon afterwards Wolsey became Lord Chancellor and rapidly made himself perhaps the most wealthy and powerful person in the country. However his downfall was imminent, and in 1529 having incurred the King's displeasure Wolsey was stripped of his riches and power. In a desperate effort to regain the King's favour Wolsey presented him with Hampton Court shortly before all his lands and goods were declared forfeit to the crown. Having been pardoned, Wolsey retired to York but in November 1530 was arrested on a charge of high treason and died whilst *en route* to London. Henry VIII then set about enlarging Hampton Court and making it one of the most luxurious palaces in his kingdom. By the time William III came to the throne, the palace was almost 200 years old and

104 Chatsworth, Derbyshire

Bess of Hardwick persuaded the second of her four husbands, Sir William Cavendish, to build a house on a terrace above the River Derwent in 1552, three years after they bought the estate. The Elizabethan house survived until almost the end of the seventeenth century, when, in 1686, the first Duke of Devonshire began to pull it down. At first he intended to rebuild only the south front, but he found building work so absorbing that once he started he could not stop. He continued to rebuild the rest of the house completing the work just before he died in 1707. William Talman was the architect of the south and east fronts whilst the west and north were designed by Thomas Archer and the Duke between them. Around the house George London and Henry Wise, the most important garden designers of the period, laid out a vast garden in the formal style of that at Versailles. Although traces of this garden and its fountains still exist, Lancelot 'Capability' Brown swept much of it away in the vogue for a 'natural' landscape. Because the gardens were laid out on a slope it was relatively easy to make features with cascades and fountains, including one (by Sir Joseph Paxton) which jets the water almost 100m (300ft) into the air. Improvements to lighten and extend the house were later made by Jeffry Wyatville but its Baroque character remains. The house is made from local stone which has weathered and mellowed to enhance the landscape in which it is built.

105 Chequers Court, Buckinghamshire

Photographed on a cold winter morning, there is no sign of life around the country residence of the British Prime Minister. This mansion is situated in the heart of the Chiltern Hills south of Aylesbury. Architecturally it is of interest as an example of a domestic building of the sixteenth century, for it was built in 1566. In 1917 Viscount Lee of Fareham presented it to the nation as a retreat where Prime Ministers could escape from the pressures of Whitehall. It has been used by a succession of premiers and their guests since 1921.

106 Syon House, Greater London

Situated alongside the River Thames, Syon was originally a nunnery founded by Henry V in 1415. After the nunnery's dissolution in 1534, the building passed to the brother of Henry VIII's third wife Jane Seymour. He converted it into a great castellated mansion. Inigo Jones is thought to have made some alterations during the seventeenth century, but it was the architect Robert Adam who between 1761 and 1770 really transformed the house, indulging his taste for Roman classicism. Most of his work was devoted to the interior decoration and is not visible in this view from the air, which does however show Syon's overall plan: round a great courtyard. It was at Syon that Henry VIII's rotting corpse was resting, *en route* to Windsor, when it burst out of its coffin and was savaged by dogs. The grounds were laid out in the 'natural' style by Lancelot 'Capability' Brown.

107 Longleat, Wiltshire

Today, Longleat is popularly known for its wildlife park which contains a number of lions and tigers introduced by the present Marquess of Bath as a tourist attraction. The enormous mansion has been the home of the Marquess of Bath and his ancestors for over 400 years. Longleat was begun for Sir John Thynne in 1568. It replaced an earlier building that was destroyed by fire. There has been considerable controversy regarding the original architect. It is likely that Thynne employed a number of architects and designers under his single unifying influence. The house represented a considerable break with traditional styles with the immense, symmetrically arranged windows looking outward, and the use of a flat roof instead of a series of ridges and gables. Sir John Thynne seems to have been a man who liked to be in fashion – Longleat was one of the first English houses to be built in a Renaissance style. Some alterations were carried out in 1807–11 by Sir Jeffry Wyatville (as he became known) who is perhaps best remembered for his work at Windsor Castle. The grounds were landscaped by 'Capability' Brown.

108 Hurst Castle, Hampshire

During Henry VIII's reign there occurred another brief interlude of castle building. The threat of a Franco–Spanish invasion following Henry VIII's breach with the Pope led him to embark on a series of castles to protect the south coast of England. Hurst Castle is built at the end of a shingle spit which juts out into the western approaches to the Solent at the point where the mainland is closest to the Isle of Wight. It was begun in 1541 and completed three years later. Its purpose was to guard the entrance to the Solent and offer protection to the ports of Southampton and Portsmouth. The castle was built of stone in the form of a central twelve-sided tower surrounded by a curtain wall on which there are three semi-circular bastions. Charles I was kept prisoner in the castle for a short time before his trial. He was brought there from Newport on the Isle of Wight on 30 November 1648. Extending outwards on two sides of the castle are two wings containing 61 granite-faced 'casemates', or gun positions, which were added in the 1860s when Britain again faced a possible threat of invasion from France.

109 Southsea Castle, Hampshire

Southsea Castle was built between 1538 and 1544 as part of Henry VIII's scheme to protect the deep-water-channel approach to Portsmouth Harbour. Within a year it saw action during the attempted invasion by the French in 1545. Despite some later additions and altera- tions, the plan of the castle is still largely original. An unusual feature is the lighthouse which still remains as a navigational aid. The castle is now used as a museum dealing with the archaeology and history of the surrounding area.

110 a & b Pendennis Castle and St Mawes Castle, Cornwall

From the Tudor period until the last century, Falmouth was one of the busiest ports in England outside London. The port was reached via a wide river estuary known as Carrick Roads which penetrates deep into southern Cornwall. The entrance to the estuary was protected on both sides by castles as part of Henry VIII's coastal defence scheme. On the west bank is Pendennis Castle situated on a high headland in a commanding position, and a mile away on the east bank is St Mawes Castle, sited on lower ground closer to the sea. Both castles were completed in 1543. Pendennis was the major fortress consisting of a central circular keep and outer curtain wall, also circular. In 1598 after a Spanish raid on Falmouth, and the threat of a second Armada, the castle was hastily strengthened, being surrounded with a large star-shaped enclosure with embrasures for cannons and a steep stone-reveted ditch around the whole of the headland. It took 400 men some 18 months to construct and they made it such an impregnable fortress that 50 years later it was the last castle to surrender during the Civil War. St Mawes Castle is more elaborately laid out than Pendennis and consists of a circular keep reached from a drawbridge on the landward side and enclosed within three semicircular towers. The keep is substantially taller than Pendennis and has a watch-tower which was very important at a time when invasion from the continent was continuously expected. Because it was designed to resist attacks from the seaward side the landward side was neglected and during the Civil War it took only one day for Cromwell's troops to take the castle without the exchange of a single shot – in marked contrast with Pendennis.

a

b

111 Bateman's, Burwash, Sussex

Bateman's was built in 1634 on the wealth generated by the flourishing Wealden iron industry. The discovery of the Midlands coal-fields brought about the decline of Wealden iron; the beautiful homes of the ironmasters became farm-houses and were eventually unin-habited. Bateman's was restored in the 1890s; in 1902 it was purchased by the writer Rudyard Kipling, and he lived here until his death in 1936. The house is a fine example of Jacobean country architecture and is made from local dressed stone. Apart from the double oasthouse added in 1770, the external appearance of the house is much the same as when it was first constructed. Kipling designed most of the for-mal gardens which can be seen to the south of the house. He wrote a number of books whilst living here, including *Puck of Pook's Hill*.

112 Uppark, Sussex

Situated high on the South Downs, Uppark was designed around 1690 by William Talman in a classical style of red brick with stone dressings. Talman was a Dutchman and Dutch influence can be seen in the design. The builder was Lord Grey of Werke who later became Earl of Tankerville; he had a chequered career, from his taking part in Monmouth's rebellion, to becoming Lord Privy Seal under William III. In 1816 the house was offered to the Duke of Wellington who declined the offer because he thought the steep hill on which it is situated would wear out his coach and horses. The writer H.G. Wells's mother worked here as a house-keeper in 1880 and Wells's recollections of Uppark are given in his autobiography. This view shows the house and stable block from the south.

113 Ham House, Richmond, Surrey

Ham House was built in 1610 by Sir Thomas Vavasour. It was later owned by William Murray, created Earl of Dysart by Charles I. The house was enlarged by Dysart and his daughter who succeeded him, as Countess of Dysart. The house reflects the baroque splendour of the Restoration period. This view is taken from the south, and shows the seventeenth-century geometric formal garden. Ham was given to the National Trust in 1948. At the same time the contents were bought by the State and placed in the care of the Victoria and Albert Museum.

115 Stourhead, Wiltshire

Stourhead, a Palladian mansion built by the banker Henry Hoare in 1718, is remarkable for its landscaped gardens which are amongst the best-known in Britain, first laid out by Hoare with the aid of the architect Henry Flitcroft. This view looks down on the lake which was formed by the amalgamation of a series of ponds. The banks were planted with trees and a path around it was devised to provide some carefully contrived views recreating the Italian landscapes painted by Claude Lorrain in the seventeenth century, in addition to incidents found in classical authors such as Virgil. A number of ornamental buildings around the lake includes replicas of Roman temples, and reveals the Georgian love of the classical style prevalent at a time when travels in Italy were becoming very fashionable. Henry Hoare's son (also named Henry) lost his wife and three children in quick succession and devoted his energies for nearly 40 years to improving the garden. The garden is still very skilfully maintained and is colourful during most seasons of the year.

114 Goodwood House, Sussex

The first Duke of Richmond, son of Charles II by his mistress, Louise de Querouaille, Duchess of Portsmouth, bought Goodwood in 1697 as a hunting box. The Charlton, the first fox-hunt formed in England, had been established near-by. The original house is hidden from view behind the main façade which was remodelled by James Wyatt around 1800. The central porticoed wing and two side wings are built of Sussex flintwork and linked by green-domed towers. At first sight this house seems to have a most unusual plan. It was originally conceived as an octagon but the money ran out before the building was even half-completed.

116 Blenheim Palace, Woodstock, Oxfordshire

Blenheim is Britain's only non-royal mansion to be called a palace. Following his victories in the Wars of the Spanish Succession, Queen Anne gave John Churchill, Duke of Marlborough, her royal estate of 2000 acres at Woodstock and arranged for Parliament to vote him a large sum of money; Churchill devoted the money to the building of the palace. John Vanbrugh was appointed the architect and the foundation stone was laid in 1705. The mansion is in the baroque style with two storeys arranged around three sides of an immense courtyard. The Duke's wife Sarah quarrelled frequently with Vanbrugh over the design. Fearing that he would be stopped before the work was completed Vanbrugh would start new parts before any single part was finished. By 1719 the East Wing was far enough advanced for the Duke to move in. Soon afterwards he was taken ill and Sarah forced Vanbrugh to resign. The Duke died soon afterwards and Sarah filed no less than 401 law suits against people connected with the building of Blenheim. The palace was completed by Hawksmoor in 1722. In spite of the problems associated with its construction, Blenheim is undoubtedly one of the finest mansions in England. Under the fourth Duke the gardens were redesigned by 'Capability' Brown who planted trees supposed to represent the disposition of troops at the Battle of Blenheim. The ornamental gardens near the house date from 1930 and are the work of the French garden designer, Achille Duchêne. Blenheim cost over £300,000, at eighteenth-century prices, to build. This view shows the palace from the south-east.

117 Audley End, Essex

Audley End is named after Sir Thomas Audley who from 1529 to 1535 was the Speaker of the Parliament which passed the Acts for the Suppression of the Monasteries. Henry VIII rewarded him with the Abbey of Walden which was subsequently demolished, a house then being built on the site. The house has been considerably altered by successive occupants. It descended to the Earl of Suffolk who in 1603 began constructing one of the largest Jacobean houses in England with buildings surrounding two great courtyards, making it more than twice its present size. Charles II acquired the house in 1669 but returned it to the Earl of Suffolk in 1701. In 1721 the seventh Earl consulted the architect Sir John Vanbrugh who advised the demolition of a large part of the building in order to make it more manageable. In 1747 the house was bought by Lady Portsmouth but it was in such a poor state that its total demolition was at one time contemplated. Much of what is visible today is the work of her nephew Lord Braybrooke who between 1762 and 1797 carried out extensive restoration. In 1763 Lancelot 'Capability' Brown was employed to landscape the grounds which can clearly be seen in this view from the west. One of the interesting features of the grounds is the monumental Corinthian temple set within a circle known as the Temple of Concord. It was erected in 1790 to commemorate George III's recovery from his first attack of mental illness.

118 Royal Naval College, Greenwich, London

These buildings close to the River Thames are notable for their symmetry and harmony of styles, although they are the work of several architects. The house in the centre at the top of the picture is known as the Queen's House. It was designed by Inigo Jones in the Palladian style for Queen Anne, wife of James I, in 1616 but two years later work was suspended. It was later resumed in 1630 for Henrietta Maria, wife of Charles I and the house was completed in 1635. The house is built of brick and faced with Portland stone. The building in the bottom right of the picture formed part of the palace designed for Charles II by John Webb, a pupil of Inigo Jones. The Great Fire of London in 1666 put a stop to further plans to expand the palace. Mary II planned to build a hospital for disabled men of the Royal Navy and after the death of William III, Sir Christopher Wren was appointed architect for the scheme. Although his talents were already stretched with the building of St Paul's Cathedral, Hampton Court Palace and some 50 gutted churches he incorporated the Queen's House and the palace into a single grand design with the assistance of Nicholas Hawksmoor and later Sir John Vanbrugh. The result is magnificent especially when viewed from the air. In 1873 the hospital became the Royal Naval College.

119 Raising the *Mary Rose*, Solent, Hampshire

On a dull Monday morning in October 1982, what remained of Henry VIII's warship the *Mary Rose* was raised off the seabed, 437 years after she had capsized and sunk in calm seas as Henry watched from the shore at Southsea. Exactly why the ship sank is not known. After several unsuccessful attempts to salvage the ship, the location was lost and in 1965 an enthusiastic group of divers led by Alexander McKee began a long search of the bed of the Solent. Late in the autumn of 1970 an oak plank and an iron gun were recovered from an area where the wreck was thought to be located. For more than a decade an archaeological excavation led by Mrs Margaret Rule proceeded on the seabed as more of the ship was gradually uncovered. Eventually the time came to lift the hull off the seabed for preservation and sub-sequent display in Portsmouth. As the crowds of spectators held their breath, the 800-tonne lifting crane, Tog Mor, slowly raised the ship to the surface. The yellow lifting frame containing the ship is just visible here beneath the surface. Above and to the right of this is the diving support ship, the *Sleipner*, which was previously used in the operation to raise the warship *Wasa* off the seabed in Sweden's Stockholm harbour.

120 HMS *Victory* and the *Mary Rose*, Portsmouth Dockyard, Hampshire

In the foreground is HMS *Victory*, Admiral Lord Nelson's flagship at the Battle of Trafalgar in 1805. The *Victory* was the fifth ship of the Royal Navy to bear her name. She was launched at Chatham in 1765 and after a successful career as a fighting ship, returned to Chatham in 1797 where, for the next three years, she was only used as a hospital ship. Then in 1803, after an extensive refit, she became the flagship of Lord Nelson. On 15 September 1805 the *Victory* left England to take part in one of the most decisive naval battles ever fought as the combined fleets of Spain and France were defeated off Cape Trafalgar. The *Victory* was badly damaged and had to be towed to Gibraltar for repairs. In 1812 she returned to Portsmouth harbour where she lay at anchor until 1922; then she was placed in the No. 2 dry dock, the site of the oldest graving dock in the world. Today the *Victory* is facing one of her greatest battles. This time her enemy is the death-watch beetle, which has caused the destruction of most of her timbers. These are gradually being replaced in an almost continuous programme of restoration. The ship continues to serve as the flagship of the Commander-in-Chief, Naval Home Command. The large white-tented structure above and to the left of the Victory covers the dock in which Henry VIII's warship *Mary Rose* was placed after her recovery from the depths of the Solent. As this photograph was taken, her timbers were being sprayed with water jets in order to prevent them drying out, pending long-term conservation measures.

121 Arundel Castle, Sussex

Arundel has been the ancestral home of the Dukes of Norfolk for over five centuries. There was a fortified structure on this site even before the Norman Conquest. The oldest part of the castle that can be seen in this photograph is the circular keep, which probably replaced an earlier timber structure, built on the castle mound or 'motte'. In 1102 the castle passed to Roger de Belleme, Earl of Shrewsbury. He began to build the stone keep, but during the same year fell out with Henry I, whose forces captured the castle after a three-month siege. After taking the castle both Henry I and Henry II continued work on the building, especially on the keep which commanded the castle from a 21m- (70ft-) high motte. During the seventeenth century Arundel saw its last siege. It was bombarded from the nearby parish church in 1643 until the garrison surrendered. When Cromwell's forces moved out in 1648 the castle was badly damaged. It was almost derelict in 1791 when the tenth Duke of Norfolk spent a vast sum of money creating a great Gothic castle from the ruins. It was rebuilt again between 1879 and 1910 when the fifteenth Duke created the great pseudo-Norman stronghold that we see today on the line of the castle bailey. In part it has a striking resemblance to the royal apartments at Windsor Castle; like Windsor, Arundel has a double bailey which can clearly be seen in this aerial photograph, together with the extensive nineteenth-century additions.

123 Osborne House, Isle of Wight

Osborne House was built for Queen Victoria at her own expense as a country retreat. She had developed a liking for the Isle of Wight having visited it as a girl. She purchased the Osborne Estate of 405 hectares (1000 acres) in 1845 but the existing house was too small. Prince Albert, the Queen's consort, designed a new house with advice from Thomas Cubitt, a famous London builder who prepared the drawings and carried out the work. The Prince saw the view over the Solent as resembling the Bay of Naples and his love of the Italian style of architecture is reflected in his design for an Italian villa. The house is rendered externally in a mortar made from Portland cement, an early use of this material, designed to provide the appearance of stone blocks. The new house was completed in 1851 and the Queen and her family spent much of their spare time here. In 1861 the Prince died at Windsor and Victoria returned to Osborne which reminded her of him. In her 40 years of widowhood everything at Osborne was unaltered as sacred to his memory and it was here that she in turn died in 1901. Today, respecting Victoria's wishes, the rooms where the Queen and Prince lived and the gardens where they walked and played with the royal children have been maintained as far as possible as they were at the time of the Prince's death.

122 Buckingham Palace, London

Buckingham Palace was built on the site of the Mulberry Garden, which was planted with mulberry trees on the orders of James I, one of whose whims was the encouragement of the growth of silk in England. It has been a royal residence since George III bought it from the Duke of Buckingham in 1762. However, it did not become the regular residence of the royal family until Queen Victoria moved in on her accession in 1837. The western façade was remodelled for George IV by John Nash, whilst the front was rebuilt just before the First World War to the designs of Sir Aston Webb. In this view the present Queen is about to depart, and sightseers have gathered at the front entrance.

124 Cliveden, Buckinghamshire

Cliveden is built on a flat hilltop overlooking the River Thames. The present house is the third to be built here, erected in 1850 by Sir Charles Barry for the Duke of Sutherland. The house is an impressive building in the classical style and is fitted skilfully onto the terraces of the earlier building, which burnt down in 1849. A former Prime Minister, Gladstone, thought highly of Barry's design and recorded his approval in a sentence, written in Latin, which is inscribed on the wall of the house below the balustrade. The grounds were designed by Lancelot 'Capability' Brown. It was in these grounds that the first performance of one of the most English of tunes, 'Rule Britannia', was given in 1740, composed by Dr Arne for the Masque of Alfred. After the 1914–18 war Cliveden developed a reputation as Viscount Astor entertained British and foreign politicians and others here – they became known as the 'Cliveden Set'.

125 Waddesdon Manor, Buckinghamshire

This country mansion was built in the 'château' style of the French Renaissance for Baron Ferdinand de Rothschild in 1874–89. It was designed by the French architect Hippolyte Destailleur to reflect in Bath stone the history of a holiday spent by the Baron and his sister Alice at châteaux in the Touraine district by the River Loire in France. The house is built on a hilltop site to the west of Aylesbury in the heart of the Buckinghamshire countryside, on land the Baron purchased from the Duke of Marlborough. Waddesdon was one of the richest country houses created during the nineteenth century. It was filled with fine eighteenth-century furniture, Sèvres porcelain, and paintings by Gainsborough, Reynolds and Rubens. Today the house and its contents are among the most valuable properties owned by the National Trust. In this view from the south-east, the way in which the landscape adds a sense of authenticity to the French architecture can readily be appreciated.

126 Lindisfarne Castle, Holy Island, Northumberland

This small castle, perched high on a rock above the sea, was first built in 1548 as a defence for the harbour of Holy Island, using stones salvaged from the nearby ruined abbey, itself founded in 635 AD. The castle was seized for the Stuarts in 1715. After the guns were removed in 1819 it fell into disuse until 1900. It was then rebuilt by Sir Edward Lutyens, who created a dream house for Edward Hudson, founder of the magazine *Country Life*.

127 Fort Purbrook, Portsmouth, Hampshire

Fort Purbrook is one of a series of artillery forts built around the naval port of Portsmouth in the 1860s to protect it from the threat of invasion by the French under Napoleon III. Although the Crimean War drew the British and French closer together there was dissension over the terms of the peace treaty and a general uneasiness that Napoleon III, emerging victorious from a war that avenged his uncle's retreat from Moscow, might similarly avenge the Battle of Waterloo. Added to this was France's supremacy in the number of newly developed iron-clad warships, the expansion of the Cherbourg docks and the coincidental development of the long-range rifled cannon which increased the range of heavy artillery to 8000 yards. It was felt that if the French were to land along the south coast of England they could bombard the dockyard at Portsmouth from the crest of the steep escarpment of the hills which overlook the town. Work on the forts began in 1860 and was carried out in the face of an immense political storm over their value. By 1868 a total of five had been constructed along the hilltop. The forts were built on what was known as the 'Prussian' system, in that each fort was capable of defending itself and the area between it and the next

fort. Fort Purbrook has been described as one of the last of the English castles. It is polygonal in plan and represents a change from the earlier bastion-type fortifications. Importantly, it is low-lying and surrounded by a deep ditch on all but the southern face (it was intended to prevent attack from the north). The main armament was mounted on the ramparts and from the central parade ground a series of tunnels led to the magazines, and to caponiers, which provided flanking fire in the ditch. It is

impossible to say whether these forts acted as any deterrent to a French invasion; such was the development in military strategy that they were obsolete even before they were completed.

128 No Man's Land Fort, Solent, Hampshire

This is one of an impressive group of sea forts constructed as part of the defence of Portsmouth (see also Plate 127). Designed to prevent the dockyard being attacked from the seaward

side, it was constructed from granite blocks. During its construction it was found from tests carried out on a wall of granite blocks that the first three shots tore up the target and the fourth destroyed it altogether. The fort was therefore hurriedly strengthened with iron and was completed in 1880 at a cost of £242,487. It consists of two tiers of casemates for 49 guns and provision on the roof of revolving turrets for five guns. In 1886 it was armed with twelve 12.5in and twelve 10in rifled muzzle-loading guns.

129 The Palm House, Kew Gardens, Surrey

The Royal Botanic Gardens at Kew were started as a hobby by Princess Augusta, the mother of George III, and her head gardener. After her death Sir Joseph Banks, President of the Royal Society, who had travelled round the world with Captain Cook, despatched people to Africa, Asia and the Pacific Islands in search of interesting plants for the collection. Queen Victoria presented Kew Gardens to the nation in 1840. It is now publicly maintained for the advancement of Botanic Science, Horticulture and Forestry. It has been responsible for the introduction of the breadfruit tree to the West Indies and the rubber tree to Malaysia. The Palm House displays almost every possible variety of palm. It was built in 1844–8 to the designs of Decimus Burton and for many years was the largest glasshouse in the world. It is over 110m (362ft) long and 20m (66ft) high and has 1260 square metres (45,000 square feet) of glass. The iron frame was prefabricated by Richard Turner at his ironworks in Dublin. The Palm House was one of the earliest in a great tradition of Victorian buildings of iron and glass, which was to include not only the Crystal Palace (now destroyed), but numerous railway stations great and small.

130 Uffington White Horse, Oxfordshire

The hill figures are a unique part of the British landcsape. The origins of most of them are obscure. The oldest, and perhaps the most artistic, is generally thought to be the White Horse of Uffington, situated on the north escarpment of the Oxfordshire Downs below the earthen ramparts of the Iron Age hillfort known as Uffington Castle. The assumption as to age is made partly on the basis of the vague resemblance of the horse to the stylized horses

on the reverse of Iron Age gold coins. The first documentary record of it however was not made until the reign of Henry II. It inspired many copies in the eighteenth century when country squires, farmers, rectors, and even doctors planned horses for hills in their neighbourhood. The scouring or cleaning of the Uffington horse, now in the care of the Department of the Environment, used to take place every seven years; it became a popular local ceremony and an opportunity for merrymaking. Thomas Hughes (of *Tom Brown's Schooldays* fame) describes the ceremony of 1857 in his novel, *The Scouring of the White Horse*. At 107m (350ft) long, it is the largest of all the white horses.

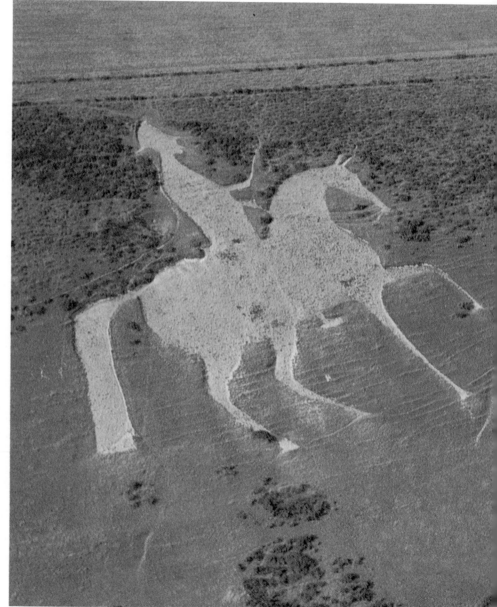

FAR LEFT

131 Westbury White Horse, Wiltshire

There were once at least nine white horses on the hillsides of Wiltshire. The white chalk rock combined with the shallowness of the topsoil made them relatively easy to cut. The Westbury horse is one of the largest, and is situated on a steep west-facing hill below the prehistoric fort known as Bratton Camp. It is the second horse to be cut on the site. It was remodelled in 1778 by Lord Abingdon's steward, restored in 1883 when the edge was reinforced with stones, and restored again in 1936 when part of the surface was covered in concrete. It is a well-shaped animal, 55.5m (182ft) long and 33m (108ft) high.

LEFT

132 Osmington Horse, Dorset

Located on a south-facing hillside overlooking the Bay of Weymouth in Dorset, this horse has the distinction of being the only one to carry a rider. It has the appearance of a statue and is supposed to represent George III riding out of Weymouth. According to the official Dorset guide, the horse had been cut in 1807 and the figure of the King was added later as a gesture of appreciation for Royal visits. However the King was offended by the fact that he appeared to be depicted riding out of a town that he had done so much to popularize! It is said that he never visited the town again. The horse is the second largest – it covers an area of almost an acre and is 79m (260ft) in length.

133 The Cerne Abbas Giant, Cerne Abbas, Dorset

Official sources describe the Cerne Abbas Giant as a representation of the Roman god Hercules, in which case it may date from around 191 AD when the Roman Emperor Commodus declared himself a reincarnation of Hercules. Together

with the Long Man of Wilmington, it is one of the largest representations of human form in the world. It is 55m (180ft) high and the club is over 30m (100ft) long. Above the giant is a rectangular enclosure known as the Trendle, which for centuries was the scene of maypole celebrations. Cerne, according to William of

Malmesbury, was the home of a particularly stubborn form of paganism. The presence of a nearby monastery casts a doubt over the authenticity of this figure. Why did the monks not destroy what must have been so blatantly pagan an object right on their doorstep? The figure was presented to the National Trust in 1920.

134 The Long Man of Wilmington, Sussex

Absolutely nothing is known for certain about the history of the Long Man of Wilmington. Once thought to be the work of the monks from a nearby priory, it is now considered to be of much greater antiquity. It has been seen as Mercury, Mohammed, a Roman soldier, the Sun God opening the doors of darkness, and even a Saxon haymaker. A possible clue to its origins was the excavation of a Saxon buckle from a grave at Finglesham near Deal in Kent in the late 1950s. The buckle has a figure which closely resembles the Long Man cast in low relief with a spear in each hand and feet pointing to the left. Perhaps there were once spearheads at the top of the Wilmington Man's staffs. In the British Museum there is a manuscript of 1779 in which the Long Man holds a rake and a staff. Its present appearance dates from 1873 when the Duke of Devonshire paid for its restoration and the figure was outlined with bricks.

135 The Whipsnade Lion, Bedfordshire

This chalk figure adorns the side of a hill below the famous zoo. It was designed by R. Brook-Greaves and cut in 1935. At first, only the outline was cut, but later more surface was removed. The lion is 147m (483ft) long and the length of the outline is 1.2km (¾-mile). The outline is preserved with a concrete edging.

137 The Clifton Suspension Bridge, Bristol, Avon

The Clifton Suspension Bridge was designed by one of the greatest Victorian engineers, Isambard Kingdom Brunel, to span the gorge of the River Avon. At one time it was the longest single-span bridge anywhere in the world. The early history of the bridge is a long saga of hopes and disappointments over a period of 35 years from 1829, when the project was first considered, until 1864, the year of its completion. Sadly Brunel never lived to see the finished bridge; shortly after watching the first steam trial of his ship *The Great Eastern* he became paralysed, and died soon after in September 1859. The bridge has a total length of 412m (1352ft) and a span between the pier centres of 214m (702ft). The road is 75m (245ft) above the water level in the bottom of the gorge. Work on the bridge began in 1836 but the money ran out; it was eventually completed using second-hand chains acquired when Brunel's Hungerford foot-bridge in London was demolished to make way for the Charing Cross railway bridge. Today the Clifton Bridge is a famous landmark and a fitting memorial to its designer.

136 Regimental Badges, Fovant, Wiltshire

The badges at Fovant were mostly cut by soldiers stationed in the area during the First World War. The first to be cut was that of the London Rifle Brigade in 1916. The idea soon caught on and other units rapidly followed this example, but because of the nearby rifle range work had to be carried out between four o'clock and seven o'clock in the morning, before firing practice commenced. In 1950 the badge of the Wiltshire Regiment (which had been worn by the local Home Guard during the war) was cut on the hill, and in 1951 that of the Royal Wiltshire Yeomanry – the most recent chalk figure in Britain.

137

139 The Royal Albert Bridge, Saltash, Devon

In 1845 the Cornwall Railway Company applied for an Act to extend the railway westwards from Plymouth to Falmouth. This involved crossing the River Tamar where it narrowed to a width of 336m (1100ft). Thus was commissioned Brunel's last and possibly greatest bridge-building achievement. The final design was produced after extensive ground-engineering investigations and work began on the site early in 1853. The overall length of the bridge is 670m (2200ft) including the curved approach spans. The main part of the bridge consists of two great wrought-iron composite prestressed trusses 139m (455ft) long. The total weight of each main part including trusses and deck is about 1060 tonnes. The trusses were of a very advanced design and have withstood not only the test of time but the ever-increasing weight of new rolling stock. The two centre spans were prefabricated on the shore, floated out on the high tide and positioned over the bridge piers in an operation personally supervised by Brunel. As the tide receded each truss lowered and rested on the pier. They were then jacked up as work proceeded on the piers, to their final position over 30m (100ft) above sea-level. On 3 May 1859 amid scenes of rejoicing the bridge was officially opened by Prince Albert but without the presence of Brunel, by this time worn out by the strain and worry brought about by the immense pressures of work, and very close to death. However, he had a last compelling urge to inspect his bridge before he died and this he accomplished lying on a couch on a specially prepared wagon of the Cornwall Railway, which was drawn slowly over the spans of this, his last great masterpiece.

138 The Humber Bridge, Yorkshire

Between its two towers the main span of the Humber Suspension Bridge measures 1410m (4625ft), over six-and-a-half times the span of Brunel's Clifton Suspension Bridge. It is the product of almost half-a-million tonnes of concrete, and 27,000 tonnes of steel. Over 71,000km (44,000 miles) of wire was used to make up the suspension cables. The Humber Bridge took nine years to construct and represents a capital investment of about 100 million pounds. Today it provides an important social and economic role, linking the communities of North and South Humberside. In this view from the north-east the far side of the Humber is almost lost in the distant haze and patchy mist. Some idea of scale can be obtained by reference to the paddle-steamer on the north bank in the centre foreground of the picture. Critics of the scheme point to the low population density of South Humberside together with the deterrent effect of tolls, and claim that the bridge will be under-utilized. In this view, taken in the morning rush-hour, only a handful of cars can indeed be seen; but it is notoriously difficult to predict future growth patterns in traffic flow.

140 S.S. *Great Britain*, Bristol, Avon

No mention of Brunel would be complete without a reference to his famous iron steamship the S.S. *Great Britain*, seen here being restored in the very dock in Bristol where she was built over 140 years ago. The keel of what was at the time the largest ship in the world was laid on 19 July 1839. It was part of a bold attempt by the Great Western Steamship Company to breach the American monopoly of the transatlantic passenger trade. The ship was launched in July 1843 and made her first voyage across the Atlantic on 26 July 1845. She covered the 5310km (3300 miles) in just over 14 days. A long and chequered career followed, during which she ran aground in Ireland; was salvaged and then used on the service between Liverpool and Melbourne, Australia; and was then used as a troopship to deal with the Indian Mutiny, after which she was sold. Her new owners took out her engine and converted her into a sailing ship. She took coal to San Francisco via Cape Horn and returned with wheat. On 6 February 1886 she left South Wales on what proved to be her last commercial voyage. Off Cape Horn a hurricane blew up and with her cargo shifting, she put back to the Falkland Islands. For 50 years she was used in the Falklands for the storage of coal and wood but in 1937 she was towed out of Port Stanley and sunk in Sparrow Cove. In 1970, after a complex salvage operation, she was brought back to Bristol and on 19 July, 127 years after her launch, returned to the dock in which she was built.

141 The Forth Bridges, Firth of Forth, Scotland

Shown here in the evening light are the Forth rail and road bridges. The rail bridge with its very distinctive shape is in the foreground. It was a masterpiece of engineering. Designed by Sir Benjamin Baker, it opened in March 1890 and cost over three million pounds at the time. It had taken 5000 men almost seven years to construct and used 55,000 tonnes of steel and 49,000 cubic metres of concrete. The total length is over 2.4km (1½ miles). It has provided a team of painters with a job for life, for when the bridge has been completely painted it is time to start all over again. Behind it is the road bridge on which construction commenced in the late 1950s. A graceful suspension bridge, it was several times the span of Brunel's at Clifton, but attracted far less attention as this type had become a fairly commonplace structure. Nevertheless it too is a superb piece of engineering, provides a vital road link across the Firth of Forth, and stands in subtle harmony with the rail bridge.

142 Tower Bridge, London

Tower Bridge is London's best-known, and also the furthest downstream of all the Thames bridges. Its centre spans can be raised to allow ships to pass to and from the Pool of London, a relatively infrequent event now that the bulk of London's dock activity has moved to Tilbury. It was designed by Sir John Wolfe Barry and Sir Horace Jones in 1886 and opened in 1894, by which time it had cost the City Corporation 1½ million pounds. The two towers are 61m (200ft) apart and 61m (200ft) high. The bridge has a total length of 268m (880ft).

143 National Westminster Bank Tower, London

Rising through 52 storeys to a height of 183m (600ft), the headquarters of the National Westminster Bank is the tallest building in Britain. It is situated in the heart of the commercial centre of the City of London, close to the Bank of England and the Stock Exchange. Designed by Richard Seifert and Partners, its plan view bears a striking resemblance to the National Westminster Bank's logo, although this subtlety of the architect's design can really only be appreciated from above. The exterior is faced with vertical stainless-steel ribs at 1.5m centres, between which are bronze-coloured spandrels and bronze-tinted glass in the windows. This gives a strong vertical emphasis to the tower and increases its apparent slenderness. The central core is a massive rigid reinforced-concrete structure capable of resisting all wind forces and supporting the cantilevered floors of composite construction, which incorporate lightweight reinforced concrete on a steel frame. It is estimated that the load of the tower is 130,000 tonnes. The tower is one of the most striking features of London's twentieth-century skyline.

144 Thames Barrier, Woolwich Reach, London

A technical innovation in the field of civil engineering, the Thames Barrier is the biggest moveable barrier in the world. It was completed in 1982 at a cost of around 450 million pounds. The south-east of England is reckoned to be sinking at the rate of 300mm (1ft) in a hundred years; add to that a general rise in tide levels, and the possibility of an intense depression centred over the North Sea causing water to be funnelled up the Thames Estuary forming a surge tide, and there is a real possibility that London could be engulfed by floodwater. In 1953 a flood in the Thames Estuary drowned 300 people and provided a dramatic warning of the threat to the City itself. Initially the threat was countered by raising the level of the river's banks but after another flood in 1971, it was realized that this was not the complete solution. After several schemes had been considered, contracts for the barrier were awarded in July 1974. The barrier consists of a series of massive concrete piers built across the river at Woolwich and linked by curved sector steel barriers which normally lie flush with the bed of the river but which can be rotated through 90 degrees to raise them into position when the possibility of flooding is imminent. There are four 61m (200ft) openings, two 30m (100ft) openings and four smaller openings for light vessels. The largest pair of steel barriers weigh 1400 tonnes each. The barrier was completed not a moment too soon; the first real test came in February 1983 when widespread flooding was successfully averted.